CONGRESSMEN
AND THEIR CONSTITUENCIES

CONGRESSMEN
AND
THEIR CONSTITUENCIES

Lewis A. Froman, Jr.
UNIVERSITY OF WISCONSIN

GREENWOOD PRESS, PUBLISHERS
WESTPORT, CONNECTICUT

Library of Congress Cataloging in Publication Data

Froman, Lewis Acrelius, 1935-
    Congressmen and their constituencies.

    Reprint of the ed. published by Rand McNally,
Chicago, in series: Rand McNally political science
series.
    Includes bibliographical references.
    1. United States. Congresses--Elections. 2. United
States. Congress--Voting. I. Title.
[JK1067.F76 1974]   328.73'07'75   74-15553
ISBN 0-8371-7820-7

RAND McNALLY
POLITICAL SCIENCE SERIES
Morton Grodzins, Advisory Editor

328.73
F931c

Originally published in 1963 by Rand McNally & Co., Chicago

Reprinted with the permission of Lewis A. Froman, Jr.

Reprinted in 1974 by Greenwood Press,
a division of Williamhouse-Regency Inc.

Library of Congress Catalog Card Number 74-15553

ISBN 0-8371-7820-7

Printed in the United States of America

For my wife, Katie

Preface

What kinds of people are likely to participate in congressional elections? How does variation in voting turnout among citizens affect other parts of the political system? What kinds of factors influence voting by congressmen? These and other questions are the topics discussed in this book.

More generally, this is a book about United States congressmen and their constituencies. We shall be concerned, in the pages that follow, with the representative process as a system of public policy-making. We shall be interested in both the election of congressmen and the ways in which congressmen are influenced in their deliberations on public policy by the constituencies from which they are elected.

Answers to the questions raised will be bolstered by data collected from all 435 congressional districts. Two sources are used extensively: *The Congressional District Data Book, Districts of the 87th Congress* (Bureau of the Census), and *The Congressional Quarterly Almanac, 1961*. These sources make it possible to describe and explain the relationships between congressmen and their constituencies in a relatively comprehensive fashion, and to test general hypotheses in a rigorous way.

We shall put to test much of the folklore concerning Congress and the representative process generally. An example is the question of whether the Senate is more liberal than the House of Representatives—and, if so, why? Another is the question of whether apathy is "good" for the political system—and, if so, why?

Various people have been instrumental in the preparation of this book. I would like to thank the Graduate Research Committee of the University of Wisconsin for salary and research support for the summer of 1962 during which most of the data for this book were compiled and organized. I also wish to thank my research assistant, Josef Burger, for his many hours of coding and machine work.

Many people have read all or part of this manuscript and have offered many helpful criticisms and suggestions. My father, Professor Lewis A. Froman, read and commented upon the entire manuscript. My debt to him increases over the years. Professor Ralph K. Huitt read the entire manuscript and offered many suggestions, especially at the beginning of my research. Chapter 1 is in part a product of my conversations with him. Professors Nelson W. Polsby, Aaron Wildavsky, Duncan MacRae, Samuel C. Patterson, Rufus P. Browning, and Herbert Jacob read and gave me suggestions on various chapters. Their comments and suggestions have made this a better book.

And finally, my wife Katie, to whom this book is dedicated, has been a constant source of ideas and solace, a rare combination.

Lewis A. Froman, Jr.
Madison, Wisconsin

Table of Contents

PART I CONGRESSIONAL ELECTIONS

PART II CONSTITUENCY INFLUENCES ON CONGRESSMEN

List of Tables

Constituency Characteristics and the Explanation of Political Behavior

Introduction

Governmental leaders must pay some attention to the preferences of the governed. This is true in every type of government, totalitarian as well as democratic. The chief characteristic distinguishing a totalitarian from a democratic government is not that the former does not listen at all to the preferences of its citizens and that the latter does. Rather, the difference lies in the number of people who are allowed to participate in the decision-making process, the range of activities in which they may participate, and their ability to influence the course of governmental policy.

In democratic societies, relatively few individuals and groups are legally disbarred from political participation, and, as compared with other forms of government, relatively few kinds of political activity, short of violence, are considered illegitimate. It is true, of course, in democratic as well as totalitarian systems, that although some groups may legally participate in politics, they are extralegally prohibited (for example, many Negroes in the South). Social constraints may be just as effective as laws in disfranchising and rendering illegitimate the political activity of some groups of people. It is also true in democracies

1

that although most individuals may legally participate, many choose not to. For example, approximately 40 per cent of the eligible adult American population does not even participate in politics to the extent of voting in presidential elections. Other forms of participation, such as voting in party primaries, working for a political party, contributing money, or contacting a congressman find even fewer participants.

However, the basic proposition remains essentially correct. In democratic systems, if people choose to participate, they are able to participate and, perhaps more important, their participation may have some impact on the course of governmental policy. Democratic systems allow citizens, through elections, political parties, and formal political institutions, to make choices and even to structure the alternatives (for example, the nomination of candidates, the making of party platforms, formation of new parties, the pressure brought by interest groups on governmental officials). Hence, participation in politics by citizens of democracies has consequences quite different from participation by citizens in totalitarian societies where choices are quite limited or even non-existent, and the kinds of activities allowed are severely restricted. Even outside of the electoral process, interest groups and other interested citizens may petition their governmental officials and hope, at least eventually, to have their preferences translated into public policy. This expectation of winning is what makes political participation meaningful and real in democratic societies.

One of the formal institutions which provides a mechanism through which people's preferences may be translated into public policy is the legislature. In all societies some system of law and order is necessary, and some type of formal institution is needed to legitimize the decisions of the active and participating elements in the society. However, legislatures, like any other political institution, are not neutral organs making laws which benefit all members of society equally. The decisions arrived at by legislatures are likely to have differential impact on citizens, depending upon their occupations, social class, race, religion, age, etc. We can expect, then, in a governmental system which provides for wide participation among its citizens, and given a political institution which distributes advantages and disadvantages somewhat unequally, that there may be some relationship between the preferences of those who participate and public policy.

This book will be primarily concerned with answering two types of questions: (1) What kinds of people are likely to participate in congressional elections in the United States? and (2) What is the relationship between the decisions made by congressmen on matters of public policy and the type of constituency from which they come? The rationale for such a study is fairly straightforward. Congress is an important law-making body in the United States. An investigation into factors which help to determine the distribution of advantages and disadvantages through congressional decision-making is therefore an important concern.

Factors Influencing Congressional Decision-Making

Members of Congress, like people in other decision-making roles, operate in a more or less uncertain world. Congressmen are confronted almost daily with the necessity of making choices on a wide range of issues and problems. Besides their activities for constituents and their own personal affairs, members of Congress are faced with an enormous number of alternative choices in the performance of their legislative function. As many as three to four thousand different bills and resolutions are introduced in Congress every session, and of these, fifteen hundred may reach the floor for debate and a vote.[1] These bills and resolutions vary from specific, local matters (such as relief for individual persons) to matters of great national and international importance (such as an education bill or foreign aid). There are also amendments to be considered to many of these bills and votes to be taken on the amendments. All this is in addition to the normal committee work which a congressman is expected to do and the many decisions which have to be made in committee.

Given the range, number, and complexity of choices to be made, how does a congressman make up his mind how to vote? What kinds of factors are influential in determining his vote?

[1] See Floyd M. Riddick, "The Eighty-Seventh Congress: First Session," *Western Political Quarterly*, XV (June, 1962), 254–74.

We can go a long way in answering these questions if we inspect just exactly what it is that Congress as an institution does and the kinds of pressures which are likely to be placed on each congressman.

First, as we have already suggested, the decisions made by Congress (when signed into law by the President) make legal and legitimate the distribution of certain advantages and disadvantages. That is, laws have certain kinds of consequences for people. For some people the consequences will be favorable, for others, unfavorable. Civil Rights legislation which attempts to benefit Negroes suffering discrimination might serve as an example. Though certain groups of people would be aided, there are others who feel that they would be hurt, economically, socially, and/or psychically by such legislation. Hence, laws usually affect different people differently, depending upon their geographic and social location in society, their occupations, their skin color, religion, etc.

This leads us to the second point, the pressures on congressmen. These pressures come in from multiple directions. Given the fact that the consequences of a law are likely to be different for different people, we would expect, on any given bill before Congress, that some people will be opposed to it, some will favor it, some will feel it does not go far enough, others will feel it goes too far, still others will want qualifying amendments, etc. On many pieces of legislation we would also expect party leaders, both in and out of Congress, to have preferences on the issue. Since party leaders have certain rewards and punishments at their disposal, they are in a position to influence the decisions of others. The President, too, is likely to be involved, as are executive agencies who must administer the program. A congressman's colleagues, especially friends, those from the same state delegation, and influential members of the committee handling the bill are also interested in the outcome of the legislation and are likely to make their preferences known. Last, but not necessarily least, a congressman himself is likely to have certain preferences about many pieces of legislation coming before Congress.

Although it may sometimes appear (especially to congressmen) that these plural pressures come from an infinite number of directions, they may be conveniently summarized in terms of five types: constituency, party, institutional, executive, and personal. Constituency pressures include written and personal contacts from the congressman's district. They also include communications from spokesmen for interest groups that are based or have affiliates within the congressman's district. Other components of constituency pressures will be discussed in the next section. By party pressures are meant stands on issues which have been taken, either nationally or locally, by members of the congressman's party. Many of these positions are ambiguous and give the party member great leeway (for example, national party platforms), but nevertheless on many issues, such as social welfare programs, the parties do take stands which may serve as constraints on congressmen's behavior.

Institutional pressures include those from a congressman's colleagues, his friends, party leaders, committee chairmen, and others who may attempt, in various ways, to help the congressman make up his mind on a particular legislative matter. These pressures can range all the way from friendly discussion to promises of help or veiled threats of withdrawing favors. Executive pressures involve a great number of factors including service by executive agencies to the congressman's constituents, provision of information to the congressman, promises of aid, cooperation, etc. Personal factors involve a congressman's own values, convictions, preferences, attitudes, and beliefs.

Many of these pressures are quite closely interwoven. For example, members of the same party are more likely to be in contact with one another than members of opposite parties. In this case, institutional factors serve to reinforce party differences.[2] Executive pressure is likely to be put more strongly on members of Congress of the President's party than on other members. Constituency pressures and party pressures are very often likely to be congruent, as we will see in a later chapter. This interweaving of pressures makes it especially difficult to make a judgment, generally, as to the relative importance of each of these factors. However, two general comments are in order.

[2] For a discussion of this in four state legislatures, see John C. Wahlke, Heinz Eulau, William Buchanan, and LeRoy C. Ferguson, *The Legislative System: Explorations in Legislative Behavior* (New York: Wiley, 1962).

First, the importance of each factor is likely to vary from issue to issue. Some bills are more "important" than others in that they affect large numbers of people, are part of the President's program, involve large sums of money, or in other ways gain widespread attention.[3] On these bills, all of the factors are likely to be operating at once, and not necessarily all in the same direction. It is on these bills that pressures from all five sources are the strongest and congressmen are often put in the most difficult conflict situations. On other issues, especially on bills and resolutions of a local nature, the congressman's own preferences, constituency pressures, and party pressures may become less important and institutional and executive factors, more important. It is on such bills that "logrolling" is most likely to take place.

Julius Turner provides evidence that these factors do vary considerably from issue to issue. Different issues had quite different consequences for party cohesion in the Congresses studied by Turner, indicating that different kinds of pressures were operating, depending upon the nature of the issue.

The results of this study of party voting in Congress on various kinds of issues can be summarized in the following table, which indicates the relative degree of party cleavage on each kind of issue, and whether the parties took relatively consistent stands on the issue through the four sessions [1921 (First Session of the 67th Congress), when the Republicans held a strong majority in the House and had returned to control of the Presidency after eight years of Democratic rule; 1930–31 (Third Session of the 71st Congress), when the Republicans held a slim majority in the House and were faltering under President Hoover; 1937 (First Session of the 75th Congress), when the Democrats, after the Roosevelt landslide of 1936, held three-quarters of the House seats but were beginning to divide on such issues as Supreme Court reform; and 1944 (Second Session of the 78th Congress), when the Democrats held nominal control of Congress and the Presidency, but the parties were so evenly divided in the House that the number of absentees determined which party held a majority at any given time].

[3] See Lewis A. Froman, Jr., *People and Politics: An Analysis of the American Political System* (Englewood Cliffs, N.J.: Prentice-Hall, 1962), chap. i, for a discussion of criteria of importance of political issues.

1. Sharp cleavage, consistent.....Tariff
   Government action
   Social and Labor
   Farm
2. Moderate cleavage, consistent...Government regulation
   Negro
   Immigration
3. Sharp cleavage, inconsistent*...Patronage
   Control of House
   Bureaucracy
   Public Works, specific
4. Moderate cleavage, inconsistent* States' Rights
   Executive and Congress
   Public Works, general
   Armament
   Foreign Affairs
   Business Claims
5. Little apparent cleavage.......Veterans and Claims
   Women's Rights
   District of Columbia
   Civil Service
   Prohibition

　* The designation "inconsistent" means that each party did not continue to support the same point of view on each roll call regardless of other circumstances. Usually such inconsistency was caused by changes in party rule, i.e., Republicans supported armament when in power, opposed it when out of office.[4]

As this quotation and table indicate, party pressures (or at least the success of party pressures) varied from issue to issue. Other factors than party were apparently influencing the votes of congressmen on many of the issues.

　Second, in the long run, perhaps the most important pressures on congressmen are constituency pressures. Merely to assert this as a generalization, however, is much easier than to prove its validity. Several of the chapters to follow will be concerned with developing supporting evidence, but a few general comments may be helpful here.

　[4] Julius Turner, *Party and Constituency: Pressures On Congress* ("The Johns Hopkins University Studies in Historical and Political Science," Series 69, No. 1 [Baltimore: The Johns Hopkins Press, 1951]), pp. 14–15, 69–70.

Congress is a highly decentralized political organization with many centers of power and many conflicting pressures.[5] Party leaders in Congress have relatively few rewards and punishments which they can employ to hold party members in line on matters of public policy. Even their ability to influence such prizes as committee assignments and leadership positions is restricted by the operation of rules of seniority and geographical representation.[6] Coupled with· relatively weak party leaders is the organization of Congress on the basis of the committee system which disperses political influence among twenty-one standing committees in the House of Representatives and seventeen standing committees in the Senate. Most of these committees also have subcommittees which, in many cases, wield considerable influence over the content of legislation.[7] Since almost all legislation is referred to committees before debate on the floor of Congress can take place, these committees are able to halt, modify, or report out unchanged legislation referred to them. This decentralized structure of Congress means that no single set of leaders is able to demand the loyalty of party adherents. Other factors, including constituency pressures, are given considerable elbowroom in which to operate.

Other important considerations affecting the influence of constituency factors are the highly decentralized character of our political party system nationally and the fact that most congressmen receive little help from the national party in their bids for election and re-election. This means that party members in Congress are relatively independent from the national party both financially and organizationally and are dependent, to a much more significant extent, on their own local district organization and financial contributors. In fact, re-election in their

[5] See Bertram M. Gross, *The Legislative Struggle* (New York: McGraw-Hill, 1953); William H. Riker, *Democracy in the United States* (New York: Macmillan, 1953), chap. v; and Roland Young, *The American Congress* (New York: Harper, 1958).

[6] George Goodwin, Jr., "The Seniority System in Congress," *American Political Science Review,* LIII (June, 1959), 412–37; and Nicholas A. Masters, "House Committee Assignments," *American Political Science Review,* LV (June, 1961), 345–58.

[7] George Goodwin, Jr., "Subcommittees: The Miniature Legislatures of Congress," *American Political Science Review,* LVI (September, 1962), 596–605.

home constituency may depend upon a certain degree of independence from policy planks in the national platform.

Also, most congressmen like their jobs and wish to remain in office. The spectre of the next election is constantly before them, and most congressmen operate on the assumption that it is dangerous (and costly) to alienate constituents back home. Hence, congressmen are likely to pay relatively close attention to constituency opinion. Much of the time, constituency pressures are probably congruent with other pressures (for example, party positions), but when there is a conflict of pressures, we can expect the conflict to be solved in favor of a congressman's constituency. The cost of ignoring such constituency pressure (defeat at the polls) is much more severe than the cost of ignoring party, executive, institutional, or even personal pressures, at least for most congressmen in most situations. Even when constituency pressures are relatively ambiguous, the cost of not paying them at least some heed may mean trouble in the next election.

The Importance of Constituency Factors

Constituency pressures on congressmen are of two kinds. First, most congressmen, in their campaigns and visits to their districts, have invited individuals and groups to contact them when the need arises. Congressmen, after all, seek votes, and one of the ways in which they do so is to be available to their constituents. The quid pro quo for such availability, in the congressman's mind, is the expectation of electoral support (such as votes, campaign contributions). Hence, congressmen are likely to receive pressure of a direct nature from constituents, including letters, telegrams, phone calls, and visits from individuals as well as interest group leaders.

Second, most congressmen are also quite well aware of the general nature of their constituency. That is, they have certain perceptions about the kinds of people who live within their districts. They would know, for example, with relative accuracy, the number of Jews, Catholics, Irish, Negroes, rich, poor, labor union members, business groups, etc. This knowledge comes with long familiarity with the people in the district, and a congressman develops a certain "feel" for what he believes his constituents want and how he, as a congressman, should vote on various issues. Hence, many congressmen probably feel that they know what is good for their constituency even in the absence of direct, overt pressure.

The importance of constituency pressures will vary, of course, from issue to issue and from congressman to congressman depending upon the nature of his constituency and his willingness to take risks. For example, midwestern legislators may not be troubled by subsidies to ship-builders (except as they cost money or demand federal attention). Eastern legislators may not be quite so concerned about reclamation projects in the Southwest. We would also expect the attention of congressmen to constituency pressures to vary with the competitiveness of the congressional districts. Some congressmen are in greater danger of being defeated at the next election than other congressmen. However, given the relative homogeneity of most congressional districts, and the variation in these districts across the entire country, we would probably find that few congressmen (and constituents) get excited about most of the legislation which passes through Congress. Most bills are relatively narrow in scope and specifically related to issues which have little relevance to most congressmen's districts.

There are certain bills, however, which demand close attention to constituency pressures by almost all congressmen. Large money bills, foreign aid, aid to education, social security, medicare, and housing are examples. These are pieces of legislation involving large sums of money and federal intervention in the economy and society which, in turn, involve many kinds of people in most congressional districts. It is these "important" bills (generally the President's "must" legislation) which gain national attention in the newspapers and which are likely to activate citizens and pressure groups on a large scale. The fact that different individuals and groups are likely to take differing positions on these issues means that conflict is likely to be intense. It is on these issues that congressmen are likely to pay most attention to constituency pressures and to have expectations about how the publics and groups within their constituencies will probably react.

If what we have been saying is true, then we would expect the behavior of congressmen to vary depending upon the kind of constituencies from which they come, especially on legislation which has national importance. This generalization is deducible from the following general theory, in summary.

Congressional districts are usually small segments of states (in the Eighty-seventh Congress only 11 congressmen out of 437 had at-large, or state-wide constituencies). These relatively homogeneous congressional districts can be described according to certain population characteristics (to be discussed below). We then find that many people within the congressional districts share roughly similar kinds of environments. This sharing of environments, coupled with the notion that many issues affect people sharing similar environments in similar ways, leads us to the conclusion that people in similar kinds of environments are likely to share similar attitudes on many matters of public policy.

We also find that these shared environments vary widely over the United States. That is, some congressional districts are predominately urban, some rural; some have large non-white populations, others small; some are rich and some are poor. Since shared attitudes about various problems confronting people are often the result of sharing similar environments, and since economic and social environments vary widely in the United States, it would not be surprising to find people located in similar environments choosing up sides in similar ways on matters of public policy, and differing with those who do not share the same environment. Nor would it be surprising to find congressmen representing different, relatively small segments of real estate, which vary in the kinds of people which are located within them, to be reflecting different points of view in their congressional activity. Since their constituencies vary, and therefore the impact of issues on their constituents varies, congressmen from different kinds of constituencies are likely to vote differently on matters of public policy, and those from similar constituencies are likely to vote in similar ways.

Since congressional districts are relatively small and homogeneous, but vary among each other on a number of characteristics (that is, are heterogeneous as a whole), and if we assume that (1) on matters of national public policy many constituents are interested in the outcomes and indicate their interest by contacting their representatives, and (2) congressmen wish to remain in office and have certain perceptions of their districts which lead them to act in such a fashion as to avoid damaging their chances of being re-elected, doing this by behaving in ways congruent with constituency pressures and their perceptions of real and potential interests within their constituencies, then we would expect variation in congressional behavior to be related to differences in constituencies. This, in a single complicated sentence, is most of the theory in summary form. It will be one of the tasks of this book to demonstrate the many ways in which constituency pressures influence the course of public policy.

One of the ways of assessing the influence of these constituency pressures is to characterize congressional districts according to average population variables. For the purposes of this study, we will focus on five gross sociological, economic, and political variables: race (percentage of the congressional district which is non-white); socioeconomic status (percentage owner-occupied dwelling units); residence (percentage urban population); population density (population per square mile); and competitiveness of the district. These factors, of course, do not exhaust the important variables which are likely to structure people's thinking about various matters of public policy and influence their political behavior. One can think of a host of other important variables, such as education, ethnicity, occupation, religion. However, these are five important variables, data on each of these variables are readily available for congressional districts, and, as we shall see, they do help us to explain differences in voting turnout among the general population, differences in roll-call voting in the House of Representatives, and other problems.

Now, let us be clear as to how we are going to use these variables. We are not saying that these gross characteristics (constituency variables) in themselves lead people or congressmen to vote one way as opposed to another. However, assuming that our assumptions above are correct, i.e., that similar kinds of environments are likely to result in similar attitudes, and assuming, in democratic systems such as the United States, the ability to organize and make demands on public officials, these gross constituency characteristics are likely to be correlated in the following ways with political behavior.

First, we are likely to find that organized groups will form on the basis of shared attitudes toward public policy.[8] That is, where environments are similar, or, putting it in the form of an example, where there is a high proportion of non-whites, we would expect that groups would form which appeal overtly to the interests of people sharing the common characteristic, especially if the sharing of that characteristic is intimately connected with public policy, as race questions are. Hence, in areas of high Negro concentration we would expect to find a number of Negro groups, some of them politically oriented such as the National Association for the Advancement of Colored People, which take up the cause of the Negro and attempt to get Negroes to vote for friends and against enemies and to lobby congressmen in their behalf.[9]

Similarly, in congressional districts with large proportions of lower status people, we would expect to find interest groups, such as labor, exposing the causes of the people who make up their membership. We are also likely to find that the size and strength of these groups will roughly correspond with the percentage of members of a congressional district who share the common characteristic. Hence, group pressure is one consequence which we might expect from examining various proportions of these sociological variables within and among congressional districts.

Second, we also find that people in general who share roughly similar kinds of environments also share similar kinds of attitudes. That is, besides the probable existence of interest groups, there will also be publics, or groupings of people who share politically relevant characteristics and who are likely to behave in similar ways politically and to differ with those who do not share these characteristics. This is especially true of voting, where many studies have suggested a relationship between certain important social characteristics and percentage of the vote for

---

[8] See David B. Truman, *The Governmental Process* (New York: Knopf, 1951), for an excellent discussion of interest groups.

[9] For an example of Negro-oriented group politics, see James Q. Wilson, *Negro Politics* (Glencoe, Ill.: Free Press, 1960).

Democrats and Republicans.[10] For example, generally speaking, men, younger voters, Catholics, Jews, Negroes, other minority groups, those in metropolitan centers, non-college-educated, skilled and unskilled blue-collar workers, union members, and low-income groups support the Democrats, while (again, generally speaking) women, older voters, Protestants, whites, those in suburban and rural areas, college-educated, professional, business or managerial, sales, non-union, and high-income groups support the Republicans.[11] Hence, publics in general who share similar economic, social, and political environments are likely to respond to political stimuli in similar ways.

Third, congressmen themselves have information and perceptions about the social, economic, and political structure of their constituencies which lead them to expect the existence of certain preferences and to anticipate certain reactions within their constituencies. That is, it is not merely direct pressure brought to bear on congressmen through interest group activity and overt public pressure to which they are likely to respond, but also indirect pressure in the form of expectations and anticipated consequences. As we have already indicated, since most congressmen wish to remain in office, they are particularly sensitive to what they think are the feelings of their constituents. Even in the absence of direct pressure, congressmen are likely to take these expectations and perceptions into account in their voting. It is also true, of course, that congressmen are themselves members of their constituencies, have probably lived there a long time, and develop a ''feel'' for how the people within the constituency are likely to react on given issues. In the absence of contrary evidence, and because a congressman does operate in such an uncertain environment where it is rarely clear to him exactly how many votes a particular action on his part will gain or cost him

[10] Paul F. Lazarsfeld, Bernard Berelson, and Hazel Gaudet, *The People's Choice* (2nd ed.; New York: Columbia University Press, 1948); Bernard Berelson, Paul F. Lazarsfeld, and William N. McPhee, *Voting* (Chicago: University of Chicago Press, 1954); and Angus Campbell, Philip E. Converse, Warren E. Miller, and Donald E. Stokes, *The American Voter* (New York: Wiley, 1960).

[11] See Seymour M. Lipset, Paul F. Lazarsfeld, Allen H. Barton, and Juan Linz, "The Psychology of Voting: An Analysis of Political Behavior," in Gardner Lindzey, ed., *The Handbook of Social Psychology* (Reading, Mass.: Addison-Wesley, 1954), II, 1124–77.

at the polls, he must often rely on these perceptions and feelings.

Hence, these gross characteristics of race, socioeconomic status, residence, population density, and competitiveness of the districts are really shorthand ways of getting at the probable existence of a number of groups, associations, and loose groupings of people (at both the pre-electoral and postelectoral stages), and congressmen's perceptions of their congressional districts. Assuming a relatively free play of these plural pressures, we would expect to find voting patterns on public policy among congressmen associated with constituency differences on these social, economic, and political variables.

Many questions of interest to political scientists come to mind which a discussion of constituency influences may help us to answer. Broadly stated, such problems would include the relationship between people's objective social characteristics and their likelihood of participating in political elections, how political institutions vary in the distribution of advantages and disadvantages and why such variation should occur, and the relationship between people's preferences and public policy. All of these questions entail problems of representation and political participation in democratic governments.

The next eight chapters are concerned with various questions of individual and legislative decision-making and how general political participation and outcomes in the legislative process are affected by various social, economic, and political factors. We will be concerned, in Part I, with factors affecting turnout in congressional and presidential elections. What kinds of constituents are more likely to vote than others? How is differential turnout related to competitiveness of the districts? How does turnout vary between presidential and mid-term elections, and what factors help us to explain instability in voting? We will then turn, in Part II, to such questions as, is the Senate more liberal than the House?, and, if so, why? What are the differences in the congressional districts of Democrats and Republicans? How important is the particular incumbent holding office in legislative roll-call votes? How does the competitiveness of the district affect who is elected and how he is likely to vote? Answers to these, and other questions, will be the focus of this study.

Part I

CONGRESSIONAL ELECTIONS

2

An Explanation of Regional and Party Differences in Voting Turnout

Introduction

One of the most important forms of political participation in democracies is voting. There are other ways, of course, in addition to voting by which members of the public may express their preferences. These include working for a candidate or party; contributing money; writing, calling, or visiting governmental officials; joining local, state, or national organizations that lobby governmental officials; and running for party or governmental office. But voting is certainly an important political act by the citizenry, and is the one political act engaged in by more people than any other. For example, in presidential elections, approximately 60 per cent of the eligible population go to the polls. Less than 10 per cent of the eligible population work for a party or candidate, contribute money, or in other ways are active politically.[1]

This chapter will be concerned with the following question: What kinds of environmental conditions within congressional districts promote participation in elections by citizens? That is, if we classify congressional districts by region of the country,

[1] See Robert E. Lane, *Political Life* (Glencoe, Ill.: Free Press, 1959).

percentage urban population, percentage non-white population, competitiveness of the districts, and other factors, will we find differences in voting rates?

We will examine differences in voting turnout among all 437 congressional districts in the presidential election of 1960, and the congressional elections of 1960 and 1958.[2] The turnout percentages are calculated on the basis of the number of people who voted in each congressional district divided by the number of people of eligible voting age within each district. Except for Alaska, Georgia, Hawaii, and Kentucky, eligible voters include all citizens twenty-one and over.[3]

In all congressional districts, of course, not all citizens of voting age are legally eligible to vote. There are also those who fail to meet residency requirements, disfranchised institutionalized populations, and, in some states, others who fail to pass literacy and poll tax requirements. Additional conditions of voting, besides age, disfranchise a small proportion of the population. Although each of these factors varies slightly from district to district, the amount of error introduced into this analysis by not taking them into account should not be very large. The difficulty of getting the necessary data on these conditions far outweighs the possible return in precision. Hence, we will include in the eligible voter pool all citizens of voting age, recognizing that some small amount of error is being introduced.

Turnout Varies by Region of the Country

The first factor to be discussed is region of the country. The 437 congressional districts were separated into the traditional categories of northern, border, and southern states. The South includes the eleven states of the Old Confederacy (Virginia, North Carolina, South Carolina, Georgia, Florida, Alabama, Missis-

[2] The usual number of congressmen is 435. However, due to the entrance of Alaska and Hawaii into the Union before the 1960 reapportionment of seats (for the 1962 congressional elections), two seats were temporarily added.

[3] Voting age is eighteen in Georgia and Kentucky, nineteen in Alaska, and twenty in Hawaii. The data for this chapter come from the *Congressional District Data Book, Districts of the 87th Congress* (U.S. Department of Commerce, Bureau of the Census [Washington, D.C.: Government Printing Office, 1961]).

sippi, Louisiana, Texas, Arkansas, and Tennessee)—106 congressional districts. The border states include Oklahoma, Missouri, West Virginia, Kentucky, and Maryland—38 congressional districts. The North includes the remainder of the states, involving 293 congressional districts.

As expected, voting turnout does vary by region of the country. Table 2.1 indicates that in each of the three elections, the northern congressional districts have the highest turnout, the southern congressional districts have the lowest turnout, and the border congressional districts lie between.

TABLE 2.1
Voting Turnout in Three Elections, by Region

Region	Turnout and Election					
	1960 President		*1960 Representative*		*1958 Representative*	
	%	N	%	N	%	N
North	72.9	(168)	69.1	(293)	53.2	(292)
Border	66.3	(30)	60.0	(38)	39.7	(38)
South	40.2	(102)	32.0	(101)	14.5	(101)

Table 2.1 also shows that within each region, voting turnout varies from a high in the 1960 presidential race to a low in the congressional mid-term election of 1958, that the variability in voting is much greater for the southern congressional districts than for the northern congressional districts, and that the border congressional districts again lie between. This election variability will concern us in Chapter 3.

Why should there be a voter turnout variation among northern, border, and southern congressional districts? The answer lies in the differences in social, economic, and political factors characterizing these three regions. Before exploring regional differences, let us first see how voting turnout varies within each region with certain social, economic, and political factors.

Relationship Between Percentage Non-White Population and Voting Turnout

Are non-whites less likely to vote than whites? Table 2.2 indicates that they are, and in all three sections of the country. The only exception is in the congressional elections of 1960 and 1958

TABLE 2.2

Voting Turnout and Non-White Population, by Region*

Proportion Non-White Population, by Region	1960 President %	N	Turnout and Election 1960 Representative %	N	1958 Representative %	N
All						
Low	75.1	(76)	73.3	(104)	55.5	(104)
Medium	67.2	(120)	65.2	(174)	48.4	(174)
High	44.3	(104)	45.2	(154)	28.1	(153)
North						
Low	75.8	(70)	73.9	(98)	56.3	(98)
Medium	72.0	(66)	70.1	(104)	54.3	(104)
High	68.8	(32)	62.9	(91)	48.4	(90)
Border						
Low	72.8	(14)	69.4	(16)	45.6	(16)
Medium	61.0	(15)	53.0	(15)	34.3	(15)
High	55.0	(1)	53.6	(7)	37.4	(7)
South						
Low	46.6	(31)	38.8	(29)	18.8	(29)
Medium	43.5	(40)	33.3	(41)	15.5	(41)
High	30.5	(31)	26.0	(31)	9.2	(31)

*In this and the following tables, the congressional districts within each region, and the congressional districts taken together (the "All" category), were divided into three groups, high, medium, and low, on each of the population characteristics to be explored. For example, in the above table, "low" means the lowest one-third (approximately) of the congressional districts on the variable "non-white population"; "medium" means the middle one-third; and "high" means the one-third of the congressional districts having the highest non-white population. Approximately one-third of the cases lie in each group. However, data were not available on voting turnout for each congressional district in some elections, especially the 1960 presidential election. The figures in parentheses are the actual number of districts in each group for which data were available. The percentages in the table represent voting turnout for each group.

in the high non-white congressional districts of the border states. It is still true, even in the border states, that the districts with the lowest non-white populations have the highest turnout; but districts with the highest non-white populations do not have the lowest turnout.

Why non-white voters in the border states should deviate slightly from the general hypothesis is not entirely clear. We can see, however, that in the border states, the exception occurs most strongly in the lowest turnout election (the 1958 mid-term election). This indicates a higher degree of stability in voting among non-whites. Non-whites are more likely to participate, relative to whites, in less exciting elections. This phenomenon will be explored further in the next chapter.

We can say, however, generally speaking, that the higher the concentration of non-whites within the congressional district, the lower the voting turnout.

Relationship Between Percentage Owner-Occupied Dwelling Units and Voting Turnout

How does voting turnout vary with a rough measure of socio-economic status (percentage owner-occupied dwelling units)? We would expect, on the basis of previous studies, to find that those districts with higher percentages of homeowners would vote in greater numbers than those with lower percentages.[4] Table 2.3 bears out this expectation.

TABLE 2.3

Voting Turnout and Owner-Occupied Dwelling Units, by Region

Owner-Occupied Dwelling Units, by Region	Turnout and Election					
	1960 President		1960 Representative		1958 Representative	
	%	N	%	N	%	N
All						
Low	41.6	(47)	52.4	(125)	37.9	(124)
Medium	60.6	(164)	57.6	(192)	40.0	(192)
High	72.9	(89)	71.5	(115)	53.3	(115)
North						
Low	65.0	(10)	62.1	(84)	49.3	(83)
Medium	72.4	(81)	70.6	(107)	53.6	(107)
High	75.0	(77)	73.3	(102)	55.9	(102)
Border						
Low	65.0	(3)	53.6	(7)	36.4	(7)
Medium	69.7	(19)	58.0	(23)	38.9	(23)
High	76.7	(6)	71.2	(8)	45.0	(8)
South						
Low	32.6	(34)	27.9	(34)	10.3	(34)
Medium	43.7	(61)	34.3	(61)	16.3	(61)
High	50.7	(7)	41.7	(6)	20.0	(6)

4 See S. Lipset, P. Lazarsfeld, A. Barton, and J. Linz, "The Psychology of Voting: An Analysis of Political Behavior," in G. Lindsey, ed., *The Handbook of Social Psychology* (Reading, Mass.: Addison-Wesley, 1954), II, 1124–77.

For each of the elections, and in each of the regions, the greater the percentage of owner-occupied dwelling units within the district, the greater the turnout.

Relationship Between Percentage Urban Population and Voting Turnout

The relationship which is usually suggested between percentage urban population and voting turnout is that the more urban an area, the greater the voting turnout. This, as can be seen from Table 2.4, is true when all the congressional districts are taken together. However, when region of the country is held constant, we find that this generalization is not true for any particular region. In the northern congressional districts, the reverse is actually true: The greater the percentage urban population, the lower the voting turnout. In the southern and border congressional districts, there is a curvilinear relationship. In the border districts, voting turnout is highest in the medium urban areas, next highest in the low urban districts, and lowest in the high urban districts. In the southern districts, turnout is highest in

TABLE 2.4

Voting Turnout and Urban Population, by Region

Urban Population, by Region	Turnout and Election					
	1960 President		1960 Representative		1958 Representative	
	%	N	%	N	%	N
All						
Low	59.8	(136)	45.7	(133)	38.4	(133)
Medium	62.6	(147)	51.3	(177)	43.4	(176)
High	64.2	(17)	52.1	(122)	47.3	(122)
North						
Low	75.3	(62)	73.0	(64)	56.4	(64)
Medium	71.5	(95)	70.8	(123)	53.5	(122)
High	70.3	(11)	64.8	(106)	50.8	(106)
Border						
Low	65.5	(13)	59.2	(13)	38.1	(13)
Medium	66.5	(13)	65.0	(13)	43.5	(13)
High	70.0	(4)	55.8	(12)	37.5	(12)
South						
Low	41.7	(36)	33.2	(33)	14.7	(33)
Medium	38.3	(36)	29.7	(34)	12.0	(34)
High	42.3	(30)	35.0	(34)	15.6	(34)

the high urban districts, next highest in the low urban districts, and lowest in the medium urban districts.

How can we account for these differences in voting turnout by percentage urban population within the three regions of the country? Why would the more rural areas have higher turnout rates in the northern districts, the medium urban and rural areas have the highest turnout rates in the border districts, and the urban districts have the highest voting turnout in the southern districts?

One factor which helps to account for these differences is a difference in the location of non-white voters within these three regions. As we have already seen, voting turnout varies inversely with the proportion of non-white residents: where the percentage non-white population is lower, voting turnout is higher. If the location of non-whites varies with percentage urban population within the three regions in a similar pattern to voting turnout, this will be grounds for saying that one reason why voting turnout varies differently with percentage urban population in each of the three regions is the fact that percentage non-white population also varies differently within the three regions. Table 2.5 shows the relationship between urban population and percentage non-white population within each region.

TABLE 2.5

Non-White Population and Urban Population, by Region

Urban Population, by Region	Non-White Population	
	%	N
North		
Low	2.42	(64)
Medium	4.47	(123)
High	14.83	(106)
Border		
Low	7.73	(13)
Medium	6.23	(13)
High	19.29	(12)
South		
Low	26.09	(36)
Medium	27.87	(36)
High	18.60	(34)

Now, an interesting set of relationships can be seen. In the northern states, voting turnout was highest in the low urban districts, next highest in the medium urban districts, and lowest in the high urban districts (Table 2.4). From Table 2.5 we see that proportion of non-whites varies in a similar pattern. The percentage of non-whites is lowest in the low urban districts, next lowest in the medium urban districts, and highest in the high urban districts. So we can say of the northern districts that voting turnout varies inversely with percentage urban partially, at least, because percentage urban varies directly with percentage non-white. That is, urban areas in the northern districts have lower turnout rates partially as a result of the fact that these same urban districts also have the highest percentage of non-whites (who vote in smaller proportions than whites).

In the border states we saw that the medium urban districts have the highest turnout rates, the low urban districts have the next highest, and the high urban districts have the lowest voting turnout (Table 2.4). Table 2.5 shows that, for border districts, the medium urban areas have the lowest percentage non-white, the low urban areas the next lowest, and the high urban districts the highest percentage of non-whites. Again, we may infer that medium urban areas have the highest turnout rates partially because they also have the lowest proportion of non-whites.

In the southern states, voting turnout was highest in the high urban districts, next highest in the low urban districts, and lowest in the medium urban districts (Table 2.4). From Table 2.5 we see that, for southern districts, the high urban districts have the lowest percentage non-white population, the low urban districts have the next lowest non-white population, and the medium urban districts have the highest proportion of non-whites. Thus, high urban areas in the southern districts have the highest turnout rates partially because they have the lowest percentage non-white population.

Table 2.6 summarizes the three sets of relationships between percentage urban, percentage non-white, and voting turnout. We see that in each region of the country, the urban category which has the highest non-white population also has the lowest turnout, the urban category with the lowest non-white population has the highest turnout, and the urban category with the middle non-

TABLE 2.6
Urban Population, Voting Turnout, and Non-White Population,
by Region

Urban Population, by Region %	Election Turnout %	Non-White Population %
North		
Low	highest	lowest
Medium	next highest	next lowest
High	lowest	highest
Border		
Low	next highest	next lowest
Medium	highest	lowest
High	lowest	highest
South		
Low	next highest	next lowest
Medium	lowest	highest
High	highest	lowest

white percentage has the middle percentage voting turnout. Hence, generally speaking, the relationship between urban population and voting turnout varies among the three regions of the country partially, at least, because the location of non-whites also varies with percentage urban among the three regions.

Relationship Between Population Density and Voting Turnout

When we take population per square mile (population density) as a predictor of voting turnout, we also find differences between northern, border, and southern congressional districts. For all the congressional districts taken together, the greater the population density, the greater the voting turnout. However, when population density and voting turnout are related separately by region, we find that only in the southern congressional districts does this overall generalization hold true. In the border congressional districts, the greater the population density, the less the voting turnout. Similarly, in the northern congressional districts, as population per square mile increases, voting turnout decreases. Table 2.7 provides the evidence for these relationships.

TABLE 2.7

Voting Turnout and Population Per Square Mile, by Region

Population per Square Mile	1960 President %	1960 President N	Turnout and Election 1960 Representative %	1960 Representative N	1958 Representative %	1958 Representative N
All						
Low	60.0	(111)	55.8	(109)	38.6	(109)
Medium	61.7	(174)	59.6	(206)	41.4	(205)
High	65.0	(15)	63.9	(117)	49.7	(117)
North						
Low	73.9	(93)	71.4	(96)	54.4	(95)
Medium	73.1	(74)	71.4	(130)	54.2	(130)
High	no data available		61.6	(67)	49.0	(67)
Border						
Low	68.6	(11)	65.0	(11)	43.2	(11)
Medium	65.0	(18)	58.2	(19)	38.7	(19)
High	65.0	(1)	57.5	(8)	37.5	(8)
South						
Low	38.6	(41)	29.3	(37)	12.6	(37)
Medium	40.1	(39)	32.4	(38)	13.7	(38)
High	44.5	(22)	37.7	(26)	18.5	(26)

Combining the evidence concerning both percentage urban and population per square mile, then, we can conclude that in the northern districts, rural, less densely populated congressional districts have higher turnout rates than urban, more densely populated areas. In the border states, medium and low urban, less densely populated congressional districts have the highest turnout rates, and in the southern states, urban, more densely populated areas are more likely to have high turnouts, although low urban areas also have relatively high turnout rates.

Relationship Between Competitiveness of Districts and Voting Turnout

We are interested, in this section, in the relationship between the level of competition for office in a congressional district and the rate of voting turnout in the district. For this purpose, the districts were divided into eight groups. On the basis of five elections for the United States House of Representatives (1952–1960), the congressional districts were placed into the following categories:[5]

Republican

1. Districts in which the Republican party won all five elections by 60 per cent or more of the vote.
2. Districts in which the Republican party won all five elections by at least 55 per cent, but less than 60 per cent, of the vote.
3. Districts in which the Republican party won all five elections, but at least one election was won by under 55 per cent of the vote.
4. Districts in which the elected representative in 1960 was a Republican, but which the Democratic party won at least once during this ten-year period.

Democratic

1. Districts in which the Democratic party won all five elections by 60 per cent or more of the vote.
2. Districts in which the Democratic party won all five elections by at least 55 per cent, but less than 60 per cent, of the vote.
3. Districts in which the Democratic party won all five elections, but at least one election was won by under 55 per cent of the vote.
4. Districts in which the elected representative in 1960 was a Democrat, but which the Republican party won at least once during this ten-year period.

For both Republicans and Democrats, the categories 1 to 4 represent a continuum from safest to most competitive. Each of these categories of district competitiveness will now be related to the average voting turnout.

As can be seen from Table 2.8, for all the congressional districts taken together there is a positive relationship, for both Republican and Democratic districts, between competitiveness of districts and voting turnout. The only exception, for the "All" category, is the least competitive Republican districts, which have

[5] *Congressional Quarterly Almanac* (Washington, D.C.: Congressional Quarterly, Inc., 1961), Vol. XVII.

a turnout rate second only to the most competitive Republican districts. This exception, which we will have reason to discuss more fully in Chapter 9, is due to the fact that the least competitive Republican districts are also the most rural districts. As we have already seen from Table 2.4, higher turnout rates are characteristic of low urban districts, particularly in the northern and border states, from which all but 5 of the 173 Republicans come.

TABLE 2.8

Voting Turnout and Competitiveness for Office, by Region and Party

Competitiveness, by Region and Party	1960 President %	N	Turnout and Election 1960 Representative %	N	1958 Representative %	N
All						
Republican						
1	72.6	(17)	72.9	(24)	52.1	(24)
2	70.9	(22)	69.8	(42)	53.1	(42)
3	71.2	(48)	69.6	(70)	52.4	(70)
4	74.7	(35)	71.8	(37)	54.7	(37)
Democratic						
1	41.1	(89)	40.4	(125)	23.8	(129)
2	57.4	(17)	55.0	(26)	38.5	(27)
3	66.8	(34)	62.5	(48)	46.4	(48)
4	71.1	(36)	69.9	(57)	53.9	(57)
North						
Republican						
1	72.1	(16)	73.3	(23)	53.3	(23)
2	72.5	(20)	71.0	(40)	54.5	(40)
3	71.0	(45)	70.6	(66)	53.5	(66)
4	75.6	(31)	72.6	(33)	55.6	(33)
Democratic						
1	75.0	(3)	59.2	(36)	47.2	(36)
2	67.0	(5)	63.6	(14)	50.0	(14)
3	72.2	(17)	69.1	(29)	53.6	(29)
4	72.9	(29)	71.3	(49)	56.2	(48)
Border						
Republican						
1	65.0	(1)	65.0	(1)	25.0	(1)
2		(0)		(0)		(0)
3	65.0	(1)	70.0	(2)	45.0	(2)
4	75.0	(3)	71.7	(3)	55.0	(3)

TABLE 2.8, con't.

Voting Turnout and Competitiveness for Office, by Region and Party

Competitive-ness, by Region and Party	1960 President %	N	Turnout and Election 1960 Representative %	N	1958 Representative %	N
Democratic						
1	63.0	(5)	53.8	(8)	33.8	(8)
2	63.0	(5)	55.0	(6)	36.7	(6)
3	67.2	(9)	59.5	(11)	40.4	(11)
4	66.7	(6)	63.6	(7)	42.1	(7)
South						
Republican						
1		(0)		(0)		(0)
2	55.0	(2)	45.0	(2)	25.0	(2)
3	35.0	(1)	35.0	(2)	25.0	(2)
4	45.0	(1)	45.0	(1)	25.0	(1)
Democratic						
1	38.4	(81)	30.8	(81)	12.4	(81)
2	46.4	(7)	35.0	(6)	13.3	(7)
3	52.5	(8)	42.5	(8)	28.8	(8)
4	45.0	(1)	45.0	(1)	25.0	(1)

When region of the country is held constant, we find, with few exceptions besides the one previously noted, in all three areas of the country a relationship between level of competitiveness for office and voting turnout. Lack of numbers for Republicans in the southern and border states, as well as lack of voting turnout data for many northern Democratic districts in the 1960 presidential election, make these figures somewhat erratic, but, generally speaking, the proposition is confirmed: the greater the competition for office, the higher the voting turnout.

We also find that competitiveness of the districts has more effect on voting turnout in Democratic constituencies than in Republican constituencies. That is, the difference in voting turnout between the least and most competitive districts is larger for the Democrats than for the Republicans. This has to do with the point to be made in the next section—that is, that Republican districts are those which have population characteristics associated with high turnout, and Democratic districts have population characteristics which are associated with low turnout. Hence, competition for office has more of an impact on districts which for other reasons would normally be relatively low in turnout than on districts which would normally be relatively high in voting turnout.

Differences in Voting Turnout Between Democrats and Republicans

As Table 2.9 indicates, in all three regions of the country and in all three elections, congressional districts which elected Democrats have lower turnout rates than do districts which elected Republicans.

TABLE 2.9

Voting Turnout and Party Affiliation of 1960 Incumbent, by Region and Party

Incumbent's Party Affiliation, by Region	Turnout and Election					
	1960 President		1960 Representative		1958 Representative	
	%	N	%	N	%	N
All						
Democratic	53.6	(178)	52.6	(259)	36.2	(258)
Republican	72.3	(122)	70.5	(173)	53.0	(173)
North						
Democratic	72.5	(56)	66.2	(131)	52.0	(130)
Republican	73.7	(112)	71.5	(162)	54.1	(162)
Border						
Democratic	65.4	(25)	58.1	(32)	38.4	(32)
Republican	71.0	(5)	70.0	(6)	46.7	(6)
South						
Democratic	40.2	(97)	31.2	(96)	14.0	(96)
Republican	45.0	(5)	41.0	(5)	25.0	(5)

This lower turnout rate by Democrats in all three sections of the country has to do with the fact that voters who elect Democrats tend to come from those areas in the three parts of the country which have social, economic, and political characteristics which are associated with low turnout. For example, in the northern states, low turnout is associated with high non-white population, low owner-occupied dwelling units, high urban population, high population per square mile, and low competitiveness

of districts. Except for the last (competitiveness of districts),
Table 2.10 illustrates that Democratic representatives, as compared with Republican representatives, come from congressional
districts with high non-white population, low owner-occupied
dwelling units, high urban population and high population per
square mile.

In the border states, low turnout is associated with high non-
white population, low owner-occupied dwelling units, high urban
population, high population per square mile, and low competitiveness of districts. Table 2.10 illustrates that Democratic representatives, as opposed to Republican representatives, in the
border states tend to come from just these low turnout areas (an
exception is percentage urban, where the Republicans, in the
border states, are from districts slightly more urban than are
Democrats).

In the southern states, low turnout is associated with high
non-white population, low owner-occupied dwelling units, medium and low urban population, low population per square mile,
and low competitiveness. Table 2.10 shows that Democratic representatives, as opposed to Republican representatives, tend to
come from districts characterized by high non-white population,

TABLE 2.10

**Constituency Characteristics and Party Affiliation of 1960 Incumbent,
by Region and Party**

Party of 1960 Incumbent, by Region	Constituency Characteristics									
	Non-White		Owner-Occupied		Urban		Population/ Sq. Mi.		2-Party in Last 10 Yrs.	
	%	N	%	N	%	N	Av.	N	%	N
North										
Democratic	12.7	(131)	54.4	(131)	79.7	(131)	12,085	(131)	28.0	(128)
Republican	3.8	(162)	67.0	(162)	65.3	(162)	1,870	(162)	20.0	(162)
Border										
Democratic	12.3	(32)	63.1	(32)	53.4	(32)	3,526	(32)	25.0	(32)
Republican	3.3	(6)	68.3	(6)	60.0	(6)	629	(6)	50.0	(6)
South										
Democratic	24.7	(101)	61.4	(101)	51.5	(101)	259	(101)	1.0	(101)
Republican	8.4	(5)	65.0	(5)	65.0	(5)	1,335	(5)	20.0	(5)

low owner-occupied dwelling units, low urban population, low population per square mile, and lower competitiveness.

In every case but two, Democratic representatives are more likely to come from congressional districts with social, economic, and political characteristics associated with low turnout. Voters from constituencies which elect Democrats have lower turnout rates than voters from constituencies which elect Republicans.

An Explanation of Regional Differences in Voting Turnout

We are now able to return to the question with which we started in this chapter, that is, voting differences in the three regions of the country. Referring back to Table 2.1, we find that northern congressional districts have the highest voting turnout, the southern congressional districts have the lowest voting rate, and the border congressional districts lie between the north and the south. These differences are now easily explained.

First, for all congressional districts, voting turnout is negatively related to percentage non-white population (Table 2.2). As Table 2.11 indicates, the North has the smallest percentage non-white population, the South the highest, and the border states lie between. Since voting turnout decreases as non-white population increases, percentage non-white population is one factor which helps to explain the smaller turnout in the southern and border states.

Second, percentage owner-occupied dwelling units is also related to turnout: The higher the proportion of owner-occupied dwelling units, the higher the turnout (Table 2.3). Do the three regions of the country vary on proportion of owner-occupied dwelling units? Table 2.11 shows that they do not. Hence, percentage owner-occupied dwelling units does not help to explain voting differences among the three regions.

Third, for all congressional districts, as percentage urban increases, so does voter turnout (although this is not true for the regions taken separately—Table 2.4). Table 2.11 indicates that the North is the most urban part of the country and that the border and southern states rank lower, in that order. Percentage urban, then, is another factor which helps to explain differential turnout by section of the country.

TABLE 2.11

Constituency Characteristics and Region

Region	Non-White		Owner-Occupied		Constituency Characteristics Urban		Population/ Sq. Mi.		2-Party in Last 10 Yrs.		Democratic Incumbent	
	%	N	%	N	%	N	Av.	N	%	N	%	N
North	7.8	(293)	61.1	(293)	71.9	(293)	7,716	(293)	28.3	(290)	44.7	(293)
Border	10.8	(38)	63.4	(38)	54.5	(38)	3,086	(38)	26.3	(38)	84.2	(38)
South	23.5	(106)	61.6	(106)	52.2	(106)	225	(106)	2.0	(106)	95.3	(106)

Fourth, for all congressional districts, as population density increases, so too does voting turnout (Table 2.7). Table 2.11 shows that the South is lowest on population per square mile, the North is the highest, and the border states lie in the middle. Since turnout increases as population density increases (when all districts are taken together), and since the northern congressional districts have larger population densities, on the average, than do the border districts, which, in turn, have larger densities than do the southern districts, population per square mile is another factor which helps to explain why turnout varies among the three regions.

Fifth, as districts become more competitive, turnout increases (Table 2.8). Table 2.11 illustrates that the northern states have the highest proportion of competitive districts, the South the smallest proportion, and again the border states lie in between. Competitiveness, then, also helps to explain differences in voting turnout among the three regions.

And last, congressional districts that elected Democratic congressmen in 1960 had lower turnout rates in all three parts of the country than did districts that elected Republicans (Table 2.9). We explained this difference in voting turnout between the parties on the basis of differences in population characteristics between the two parties and the fact that Democratic districts were more likely than were Republican districts to have population characteristics associated with low turnout. We would expect, then, that the section of the country with the highest proportion of Democratic representatives would also be the section with the lowest turnout, the section of the country with the next highest proportion of Democrats would be the next lowest in voting turnout, and the section of the country with the smallest proportion of Democrats would have the highest voting turnout. Table 2.11 shows this to be the case also.

To recapitulate the findings in this section, then, among all congressional districts, low turnout is directly related to high non-white population, low owner-occupied dwelling units, low urban population, low population per square mile, low competitiveness for office, and high proportion of Democrats. The three regions of the country vary in turnout from highest to lowest in the following order: northern, border, southern. The three regions of the country also vary on each of these characteristics (except owner-occupied dwelling units) in such a way that characteristics associated with low turnout are also more prevalent in the South than in the border states, and more prevalent in the border states than in the North. We may conclude, then, that regional differences in voting turnout may be explained, at least partially, on the basis of differences in population characteristics.

Summary and Conclusions

Five social, economic, and political factors have been used in this chapter to explain differences in voting turnout in the northern, border, and southern congressional districts, and between Democrats and Republicans. It would now, perhaps, be useful to summarize the major findings in this chapter.

For all congressional districts, the following propositions were found to be true:

1. The greater the percentage non-white population, the smaller the voting turnout.
2. The smaller the percentage owner-occupied dwelling units, the smaller the voting turnout.
3. The smaller the percentage urban population, the smaller the voting turnout.
4. The lower the population per square mile, the lower the voting turnout.
5. The less competitive the district, the lower the voting turnout.
6. Democratic districts have smaller voting turnouts than do Republican districts.

Five of these six propositions help to explain why northern congressional districts have higher rates of voting than do border districts and why border districts have higher rates than do southern districts. Northern districts have higher proportions of urban, densely populated, competitive, Republican districts, and a lower proportion of non-whites (all characteristics leading to higher turnout when all congressional districts are taken together) than do border districts; and border districts, in turn, stand in the same relationship with southern districts. The sections of the country do not differ on percentage owner-occupied dwelling units.

Taking each section of the country separately, we found the following propositions to be true:

For the northern congressional districts:

1. The greater the percentage non-white population, the smaller the voting turnout.
2. The smaller the percentage owner-occupied dwelling units, the smaller the voting turnout.
3. The higher the percentage urban population, the smaller the voting turnout.
4. The higher the population per square mile, the lower the voting turnout.
5. The less competitive the district, the lower the voting turnout.
6. Democratic districts have smaller voting turnout rates than do Republican districts.

Proposition 6 was explained on the basis of the fact that Democratic districts, as compared with Republican districts, are relatively more non-white in population, have a lower percentage owner-occupied dwelling units, are more urban, and more densely populated, all factors related to low turnout in the North. Running counter to this explanation was the fact that Democratic districts are more competitive than Republican districts. This more competitive nature of the Democratic districts in the North may help explain why differences in turnout between Democratic and Republican congressional districts in the North are less than in either the border or southern states.

For the border congressional districts:

1. The greater the percentage non-white population, the smaller the voting turnout.
2. The smaller the percentage owner-occupied dwelling units, the smaller the voting turnout.
3. The higher the percentage urban population, the smaller the voting turnout. However, middle urban districts have higher turnout rates than do the lowest urban districts.
4. The higher the population per square mile, the lower the voting turnout.

5. The less competitive the district, the lower the voting turnout.

6. Democratic districts have smaller voting turnout rates than do Republican districts.

Again, proposition 6 was explained on the basis of the fact that Democratic districts, as compared with Republican districts, are relatively more non-white in population, have a lower percentage owner-occupied dwelling units, are more densely populated, and are less competitive, all factors related to low turnout in the border states. However, contrary to the prediction, Republican districts are slightly more urban than Democratic districts.

For the southern congressional districts:

1. The greater the percentage non-white population, the smaller the voting turnout.

2. The smaller the percentage owner-occupied dwelling units, the smaller the voting turnout.

3. The lower the percentage urban population, the smaller the voting turnout. However, middle urban districts have lower turnout rates than do the lowest urban districts, interpreted as resulting from the higher proportion of Negro voters in the middle urban districts.

4. The lower the population per square mile, the lower the voting turnout.

5. The less competitive the district, the lower the voting turnout.

6. Democratic districts have smaller voting turnout rates than do Republican districts.

Proposition 6 was explained on the basis of the fact that Democratic districts in the South, as compared with Republican districts, are relatively more non-white in population, lower in percentage owner-occupied dwelling units, less urban, less densely populated, and less competitive, all factors which lead to low turnout in the South.

With two exceptions (competitiveness in the northern states and urbanness in the border states), then, characteristics associated with low turnout in each of the regions of the country were also associated with the party with the lowest rates of turnout, that is, the Democratic party.

Two factors showed a different relationship in the three regions. In the North, high urbanness and high population density were associated with low turnout. In the border states, high urbanness and high population density were also associated with low turnout, except that the middle urban districts had the highest turnout. In the South, low urbanness and low population density were associated with low turnout. These differences were partially explained on the basis of the location of non-whites within these three regions of the country. In the North, non-whites are located predominately in the urban areas. This is less true of the border states, where non-whites are predominately in urban areas, and, next, in the most rural areas. In the southern states, non-whites are predominately in middle urban and low urban areas. Since non-whites have lower turnout rates in all three sections of the country, where they are located is an important factor in explaining differences in urban-rural voting turnout in the three sections.

3

Some Implications of Voting Instability

Introduction

One of the questions which has traditionally interested political scientists is why some countries have stable governments and some have unstable governments. This interest has led investigators into a host of possible "causal" factors relating the kind of people being governed (such as their values, attitudes, beliefs, level of consensus on the "rules of the game") and the type of governmental decision-making apparatus within the country. In democratic systems, and in the United States in particular, researchers have focused on the relationships among the preferences of citizens, whose preferences are likely to get translated into public policy, and the type of decision-making process involved. The reason for such a focus is relatively self-evident: if a government which allows for the articulation of preferences and participation in the decision-making process by its citizens is to be stable, then there must be some relationship between the preferences of the governed, especially intense preferences shared by large groups of people, and public policy. If widely shared, intense preferences are not satisfied, this would be one possible cause of governmental instability.

But the satisfaction of people's substantive preferences is not the only factor which affects stability of the government. As it

turns out, very often relatively widely shared, intense preferences may be thwarted without the consequences of political up-
heaval. The explanation lies in what some researchers have called
"consensus on democratic norms." That is, not only do people
have preferences as to what public policies they prefer (substantive or "content" preferences), they also have preferences
as to how such preferences should be implemented ("process"
preferences). Hence, consensus or widespread agreement on
decision-making norms or rules can act as a constraint on people's
behavior, especially those people who are being frustrated in
their attempts to satisfy certain content preferences. In the pursuit of these substantive preferences, if people are willing to
abide by "the rules of the game," and if these rules prescribe
non-violent, patient participation, stability of government will
be enhanced.

It is thought by some that political stability in the United
States is promoted by the widespread acceptance of democratic
norms among the general population. If certain groups or publics
pursued their content preferences in such a way as to violate
widely shared process preferences (or democratic norms), they
would be held in check by a countervailing power of groups in
the general public who become aroused by these violations. Such
is the theory propounded, for example, in David Truman's *The
Governmental Process*. Truman suggests that groups who break
the widely shared democratic norms will activate dormant, "potential groups" who will rise to the occasion and smite the
violators.[1]

Recent research, however, casts some doubt on this theory of
stability. Although it has long been known that people's content
preferences vary depending upon their objective and subjective
environmental experiences (Chapters 2 and 7 attempt to illustrate this point in a concrete fashion), it has not been known,
until recently, that their process preferences also vary. That is,
although there might be said to be a relatively wide consensus in
the United States on abstract goals of democratic decision-
making, there is less agreement on how concrete situations should
be handled within the pursuit of these goals.[2] There is a possi-

---

[1] David B. Truman, *The Governmental Process* (New York: Knopf, 1951).
[2] Robert A. Dahl, *Who Governs?* (New Haven: Yale University Press,
1961), chap. xxviii.

bility for wide interpretation of the abstract goals within any given situation.

Second, not all groups share the democratic goals equally. As Herbert McClosky pointedly brings home, lower status groups are much less likely to share in the democratic norms of majority rule, tolerance of differences of opinion, protection of minority rights, First Amendment freedoms of speech, assembly, and religion, and others.[3] These lower status groups include the economically poorer, less educated people in the United States. Seymour Martin Lipset also suggests that the lower classes are likely to have more authoritarian values,[4] and Samuel Stouffer presents evidence to indicate that political leaders (generally of higher status than non-leaders) are more likely to subscribe to democratic norms of tolerance of minority opinions than are non-leaders.[5]

The earlier theory of the general public defending the democratic norms through the aroused activity of potential interest groups, then, needs some revision. Apparently, it is among the better educated, middle and upper classes that the democratic norms are most widespread, and it is this strata of society which may hold in check the outbursts of antidemocratic behavior of the less educated, lower classes.

These recent findings have certain consequences for a theory of political stability in the United States. It has long been known, for example, that political participation in the United States varies considerably among the population. Higher status groups, in general, are more likely to participate than lower status groups. That is, the economically better off, better educated, higher occupational groups are more likely to participate in politics than are their opposites.[6]

[3] Herbert McClosky, "Ideology and Consensus in American Politics," Paper delivered at the 1962 Annual Meeting of the American Political Science Association, Washington, D.C., September, 1962.

[4] Seymour Martin Lipset, *Political Man* (Garden City, N.Y.: Doubleday, 1960), p. 32.

[5] Samuel A. Stouffer, *Communism, Conformity, and Civil Liberties* (New York: Doubleday, 1955).

[6] Bernard Berelson, Paul F. Lazarsfeld, and William N. McPhee, *Voting* (Chicago: University of Chicago Press, 1954); Angus Campbell, Gerald Gurin, and Warren E. Miller, *The Voter Decides* (Evanston, Ill.: Row, Peterson, 1954); Angus Campbell, Philip Converse, Warren E. Miller, and Donald Stokes, *The American Voter* (New York: Wiley, 1960).

Under the older theory of widely shared consensus on democratic rules among all strata of society, political apathy was considered to be "good" in democratic decision-making. For example, as Berelson, Lazarsfeld, and McPhee argue, political apathy means that there is less likely to be political instability.[7] The reason lies in the following argument.

In the United States there are approximately 100 million eligible voters. If only 60 per cent (or 60 million) of these eligible voters vote in presidential elections, and the vote splits 55 per cent for the winner (or 33 million votes) and 45 per cent for the loser (or 27 million), then only 27 million voters *lost*. The apathetic, non-voter, although he did not win, did not lose either. And, since he did not participate, he may be considered to be willing to acquiesce in any decision. That is, the election was not important enough for him to bother to vote, and he may be considered to be little concerned with the outcome.

If, however, all 100 million vote, and the vote splits 55 per cent (or 55 million) to 45 per cent (or 45 million), then 45 million people lost rather than 27 million. The more losers there are, the more trouble for the stability of the political system. Add to this the fact that an election in which voluntary participation is high may also mean that people's preferences are intense and there is strong concern over who wins. This situation, with a large number of intense losers, presents an increased possibility of political instability. Apathy, or non-participation, therefore, is good because it reduces the chances for such instability.

When one considers the recent findings with regard to consensus on the democratic norms—that is, that consensus varies directly with status—and combines this generalization with the findings that upper status people (better educated, wealthier, higher occupational groups) are more likely to participate in the democratic process, then apathy carries with it mixed blessings. The active participators, including the voters, are more likely to share the democratic norms than are those who do not participate, but this leaves a large number of people who may be potentially activated into political activity and who do not share the democratic norms to the same extent. These apathetic people are

[7] Berelson *et al.*, *op. cit.*, chap. xiv.

less likely to identify with a political party[8] and so are more subject to the efforts of non-democratic leaders to mobilize them in ad hoc groups. During periods of crisis, this reservoir of apathetic, potentially non-democratic people is a potential threat to the stability of the political system.

What are the voting patterns of relatively apathetic groups? Although the data to be presented in this chapter are limited by the lack of an election in what would generally be considered to be a crisis period, we can look at the voting patterns of constituencies with potentially unstable voters to see how they differ in their rates of voting turnout from constituencies with potentially stable voters. We will be concerned, essentially, with differences in rates of turnout between the 1958 and 1960 congressional elections.

Instability in Voting

The first observation to be made has already been suggested in Chapter 2, that is, voting turnout varies from election to election. Turnout is highest in presidential elections, next highest in congressional elections in presidential years, and lowest in congressional mid-term elections (Table 3.1). To the extent that the unstable voters could make up a sizeable proportion of the electorate, then, crisis periods, in activating the unstable voters, should affect congressional elections in mid-term years more than in presidential years or presidential elections. This means that if we can expect demagogy and non-democratic behavior by elected officials and those seeking elective office at all in the United States, we can expect it in areas where turnout is lowest in "normal" elections. We can expect demagogy from congressmen and senators rather than from Presidents, especially those congressmen and senators elected in mid-term elections. It is in these low turnout elections that demagogues would find it easier to mobilize the necessary support to win.

Table 3.1 also shows that voting turnout varies with section of the country. The lowest turnout is in the southern congressional districts in all three elections, reaching as low as 14.5 per cent in

---

[8] Berelson *et al.*, *op. cit.*; Campbell *et al.*, *op. cit.*; and Campbell *et al.*, *op. cit.*

TABLE 3.1

Voting Turnout in Three Elections, by Region

Region	Turnout and Election					
	1960 President		1960 Representative		1958 Representative	
	%	N	%	N	%	N
North	72.9	(168)	69.1	(293)	53.2	(292)
Border	66.3	(30)	60.0	(38)	39.7	(38)
South	40.2	(102)	32.0	(101)	14.5	(101)

the 1958 congressional elections. Voting turnout is next lowest in the border congressional districts, and highest in the northern districts.

If it is true that crisis situations are likely to result in instability, then we would predict two additional consequences from the data in Table 3.1. First, since voting turnout is lower in the South than in the border and northern states, we would predict greater likelihood of instability and manifestations of instability such as demagogy in areas like the South where turnout during "normal" periods is so low. Demagogy has, in fact, been more prevalent in the South than in other areas of the country, but much of the reason has been attributed to the fact that it is, essentially, a one-party area. There are, of course, other one-party areas in the northern and border states which are not so subject to the rise of demagogic leaders. Part of this undoubtedly has to do with the higher proportions of Negroes in the South and southern attitudes in regard to the Negro, but it may also be due to the fact that instability in voting is facilitated by the normally low turnout rates which exist in the South in most elections.[9]

Second, we would predict demagogy in congressional elections more than in presidential elections, and especially in mid-term elections where the normal turnout is only about 15 per cent. We would also expect demagogy to be related to percentage non-white population.

However, there is some evidence to indicate, at least during relatively normal periods, that instability in political participation (as measured by voting) is more characteristic of those

[9] See V. O. Key, Jr., *Southern Politics in State and Nation* (New York: Knopf, 1949) for an excellent analysis of the politics of southern states.

groups which we would expect to be more in tune with democratic norms than those groups which we would expect to be less strong in their democratic process preferences. For example, on the basis of the previous discussion, we would expect constituencies with high non-white populations to be more unstable in their voting than constituencies with low proportions of non-whites. We would also expect congressional districts with relatively large numbers of poor people (as measured by low owner-occupancy of dwelling units) to be more unstable in their voting than those districts with more well-to-do constituents. These constituencies would contain the poorer, less educated groups which we would expect, according to McClosky, Stouffer, and Lipset, to be less strongly imbued with democratic norms.

Table 3.2 indicates, however, that in each section of the country it is the more highly non-white, less well-to-do constituencies that have the most stability in voting from election to election. Although, as we saw from the last chapter, their turnout rates are lower, they are more constant from election to election.

This, then, would be indirect evidence to indicate that, at least during relatively normal periods, instability in voting is not more characteristic of low turnout groups (the less well integrated groups such as non-whites, the less well-to-do, the less well educated). This evidence, at least by inference, undercuts the

TABLE 3.2

Differences in Voting in the 1960 and 1958 Congressional Elections and Non-White Population and Owner-Occupied Dwelling Units

Percentage Non-White, Owner-Occupied	Percentage Differences in Voting in 1960 and 1958, by Region					
	North		Border		South	
	%	N	%	N	%	N
Non-White						
Low	17.6	(98)	23.8	(16)	20.0	(29)
Medium	15.8	(104)	18.7	(15)	17.8	(41)
High	14.5	(91)	16.2	(7)	16.8	(31)
Owner-Occupied Dwelling Units						
Low	12.8	(82)	17.2	(7)	17.6	(34)
Medium	16.7	(105)	19.1	(23)	18.0	(61)
High	17.6	(100)	26.2	(8)	21.7	(7)

notion that less democratically oriented groups are more unstable than more democratically oriented ones. Apparently what is happening is this. These low turnout groups are relatively immune to political forces. From other evidence, we can infer that poorer, less well educated groups are less likely to be interested in political events, less knowledgeable about them, and have less feeling that participation will accomplish anything.[10] They are also groups which are more difficult to reach with political communications.[11] They are less committed to a political party, less likely to come into contact with political news, and are less likely to attend campaign rallies, watch political events on television, or in other ways come into contact with political affairs. They are, in a sense, insulated from politics. For these reasons, their voting patterns are likely not only to be low, but to be relatively constant at a low rate.

Now, the big unanswered question in this discussion is whether crisis situations (war, depression) would find these less integrated groups turning out in large numbers. My tentative guess would be no. On the basis of the findings presented here, and the discussion of other research findings, one could generalize in this fashion: Lower status groups are more likely to be nondemocratic in their value orientations, but are also less likely to participate in the political process. This lower participation rate is due to insulation from the political process and the difficulty of reaching these potential voters through the mass media and other communication processes. Because of this insulation from politics, the lower status, less democratically oriented groups are more difficult to mobilize, perhaps even during crisis situations, and hence they are relatively stable in their voting patterns (or non-voting patterns). Even during crisis periods, we would not expect these low participators to shake off their lethargy. Or at least, we would expect that they would probably be the last groups to do so.

These inferences, then, mean that fears that apathy might create political instability during crisis situations because the non-democratic voter would be more likely to participate in the

[10] Robert E. Lane, *Political Life* (Glencoe, Ill.: Free Press, 1959).
[11] Joseph T. Klapper, *The Effects of Mass Communication* (Glencoe, Ill.: Free Press, 1960).

political process are probably unfounded. The less-democratically oriented voter is not likely to participate under any circumstances because of his insulation from the political world. Hence we can, I think, at least tentatively agree with Berelson, Lazarsfeld, and McPhee cited earlier.[12] Apathy is probably good for the political system in that it is conducive to overall stability. The person who is less likely to vote is the person who is less well integrated into the political community and the person who is less likely to share in the democratic norms. It does not appear that his voting is any more unstable than others. If anything, he is more stable in his participation, although at a relatively low rate.

[12] Berelson *et al.*, *op. cit.*, chap. xiv.

4

The Importance of the Setting in Election Campaigns

Introduction

Election campaigns serve multiple functions in the American political system, but two functions stand out most clearly. For the potential voters, the campaign provides an opportunity to get to know the candidates who are running for office. Many people, of course, show no interest in politics in general, or campaigns in particular, and hence do not pay attention to the activities of the candidates. Even during presidential campaigns, only about one-third of the adult Americans indicate that they are very much interested in following the political campaigns. Another one-third say they are somewhat interested, and from one-quarter to one-third indicate no interest at all.[1] Those who are interested and concerned are more likely to think of themselves as belonging to a political party and are more likely to vote in the election.[2] Interested and concerned potential voters may get the opportunity during the campaign to find out what the incumbent has been doing during his term of office and what the challenger promises to do.

[1] Angus Campbell, Gerald Gurin, and Warren E. Miller, *The Voter Decides* (Evanston, Ill.: Row, Peterson, 1954), p. 33.
[2] Angus Campbell, Philip E. Converse, Warren E. Miller, and Donald E. Stokes, *The American Voter* (New York: Wiley, 1960), pp. 103, 144.

50

Perhaps more important for voters, the campaign provides an opportunity for them to get involved in political events and situations and, in the election, to support the party and candidate of their choice. For most voters, the campaign is a mechanism through which they may reinforce their own predispositions to vote for one party's candidate or the other.

The second important function which election campaigns serve is to provide the candidates with the opportunity to activate their party following and latent supporters in the hopes of getting them to the polls on election day. During the campaign period, the candidates can try to stimulate voters into voting for them. In short, it is during the election campaign that an incumbent congressman is called upon to justify his record in Congress. It is during the campaign that the candidates, incumbents as well as challengers, have an opportunity to fashion a coalition of publics and groups in the attempt to get more votes than their opponents. It is during the campaign that Democratic candidates attempt to get the potential Democrats to the polls and Republican candidates attempt to get the potential Republicans to the polls. And it is at the end of the campaign, the election, that the eligible voters in a congressional district have the opportunity to choose among the alternative candidates.

We will attempt, in this chapter, to discuss factors which influence the outcome of elections. More particularly, we will try to demonstrate the importance that party affiliations play in elections and the difficulty candidates face in manipulating the outcome during their campaigns. Our discussion, it is hoped, will help to answer a very important and practical question: Given a particular congressional constituency, what kinds of electoral strategies and tactics are available to the candidates in their campaigns?

This discussion will begin from the basic premise that a candidate is severely constrained in his attempt to control the outcome of his campaign. That is, what is more important than the candidate's activities is the setting in which the campaign takes place. Many of the activities of candidates will be ineffective in increasing the probability of winning because of the structure of the setting itself.

Of all the factors involved in the setting which may impinge upon an election, by far the most important is the number of Democrats and Republicans in the electorate. Voting study after voting study has shown that at least 75 per cent of the American electorate identify with one of the major political parties and that these identifications are relatively stable and lasting.[3] As we have already seen, the interested and concerned potential voter is more likely than the less interested to identify with a political party. Those interested and concerned party identifiers are also more likely to expose themselves to campaign communications such as television, radio, and newspapers. And, perhaps most important of all, they are also more likely to vote. Being already predisposed to vote for the candidates of one party or the other, it takes some doing to get them to change their minds during the course of a campaign.

Other factors in the setting (the two most important being the appeal of the candidate himself as a person, and issues) may be treated as supporting or running counter to party preferences.[4] That is, occasionally it may occur that the personal appeal of the candidate of the opposite party, or a particular issue which is important to the voter, will be strong enough to dissuade him from voting for the candidate of the party he normally prefers and attract him to the candidate of the opposition party. Such, for example, happened in the 1952 and 1956 presidential elections, when many "normal" Democrats were attracted to vote for the Republican candidate because of his personal appeal.[5]

It is usually the case, however, that party, issues, and candidates push the voters in the same direction. That is, those who identify with a political party are predisposed to look favorably upon the candidate of the party and to agree with the stands on issues which the party takes. In fact, voters will even see the party as taking the same positions on issues as they themselves do even when this is not the case.[6]

These other factors in the setting (candidate appeal, and

---

[3] Bernard Berelson, Paul F. Lazarsfeld, and William N. McPhee, *Voting* (Chicago: University of Chicago Press, 1954), Campbell *et al.*, *The Voter Decides, op. cit.*, and Campbell *et al.*, *The American Voter, op. cit.*
[4] See Angus Campbell *et al.*, *The Voter Decides, op. cit.*
[5] Angus Campbell *et al.*, *The American Voter, op. cit.*, chap. iii.
[6] Bernard Berelson *et al.*, *op. cit.*

issues) are also more unique than party identification in that they are likely to vary considerably from election to election. In analyzing the role of campaigns in elections, then, it is important to include either survey data or election statistics illustrating the basic pool of supporters each candidate has to draw upon. Other factors in the setting can then be analyzed in the attempt to gauge their impact on the party loyalties of the voters.

Predicting an Election

The proposition that candidates have little control over the outcome of elections becomes less true under two conditions: (1) The more competitive the district, the more impact the campaign can have on the outcome; and (2) The greater the inequality of resources of the candidates, the greater the control over the outcome by the candidate with the greater resources (resources include, among other things, money, time, energy, and organization). These qualifying conditions are additive, i.e., as the district becomes more competitive, inequality of resources becomes more important. What we will attempt to do in this analysis is to demonstrate the feasibility of this argument by a case study of Democratic Representative Robert W. Kastenmeier's congressional district (the Second Congressional District of Wisconsin). We will attempt to identify the factors which make Kastenmeier's re-election highly probable.[7]

The argument will run like this: There are more Democrats than Republicans in the Second District of Wisconsin. Also, there are factors present which indicate that the percentage of Democrats is increasing. Both candidates are approximately equal in resources, and there are no other factors (such as an attractive Republican candidate for President or a charge of malfeasance in office against Kastenmeier) which will upset the party ratio. Under these conditions, there is little either candidate can do to control the re-election of Kastenmeier. But first, we must dispose of the two qualifying conditions as stated above having to do with equality of resources and competitiveness of the district.

[7] The election referred to took place in November, 1962. An earlier draft of this chapter was written in the summer of 1962.

First, we will assume (on the basis of casual evidence) that Kastenmeier's opponent, Ivan Kindshi, and Kastenmeier himself are approximately equal in resources. Both are young, active, experienced politicians with party organizations and party money behind them. At least there is no reason to assume that their political resources are greatly different. We can expect, from both, a vigorous campaign. Second, although on the surface the Second Congressional District of Wisconsin appears to be highly competitive, it is not. The evidence for this assertion follows.

Representative Kastenmeier was elected to Congress in 1958 by defeating the incumbent Republican Representative Donald E. Tewes. Kastenmeier is the second Democrat to be elected from the Second District since it was first formed after the 1930 census (the other Democrat was elected in 1932 and served only one term). In 1960, Kastenmeier was re-elected, again defeating Tewes. The percentage of the two-party vote for the Democratic candidate has been, since 1952, 37.1 (1952), 46.0 (1954), 44.7 (1956), 52.1 (1958), and 53.4 (1960). What these figures indicate is that the Second District has changed from strong Republican to weak Democrat. What we have to answer now is (1) why?, and (2) will it at least continue to maintain itself at this level (and possibly even change to strong Democrat)? The answer to the second question is that the Second District will at least continue to be 52 to 54 per cent Democratic, and possibly will even go higher (barring "unusual events," to be discussed below). Now to answer the "why" question.

The Second District of Wisconsin is composed of five counties. Relevant census data for these five counties are presented in Table 4.1. As Table 4.1 illustrates, there is a wide variation in population changes among the five counties. Dane (including the city of Madison) and Waukesha (bordering Milwaukee County) are by far the two largest counties in population, are increasing in population fastest, and are becoming more urban more quickly than the other three counties. But what is perhaps more interesting is the increase in Democratic vote corresponding with these population changes. Table 4.2 presents these data.

Table 4.2 illustrates a host of interesting generalizations. Using 1948 as the base year, each county dropped in Democratic

TABLE 4.1

Population Characteristics for the Five Counties in the Second District of Wisconsin*

County	Number N	Increase since 1950 %	Urban %	Urban Increase since 1950 %	Rural Increase since 1950 %
			Population Characteristics		
Columbia	36,708	7.9	30.8	6.7	8.4
Dane	222,095	31.1	75.4	45.6	0.6
Dodge	63,170	9.6	46.8	16.2	4.5
Jefferson	50,094	16.3	50.7	17.1	15.5
Waukesha	158,249	84.2	65.1	253.5	—2.7

*Data compiled from *1960 Census of Population* (U.S. Department of Commerce, Bureau of the Census [Washington, D.C.: Government Printing Office, 1961]).

TABLE 4.2

Democratic Vote for the Five Counties in the Second District of Wisconsin in Seven Elections for the House of Representatives

County	1948 %	1950 %	1952 %	1954 %	1956 %	1958 %	1960 %
			Democratic Vote, Election Years				
Columbia	35.8	35.7	26.9	38.1	36.2	46.2	45.3
Dane	58.6	54.9	49.1	56.9	54.8	60.9	63.1
Dodge	34.9	29.2	23.6	34.1	38.7	45.1	46.4
Jefferson	38.9	34.3	28.9	39.1	41.1	49.8	48.9
Waukesha	35.2	32.6	31.3	39.2	36.0	44.1	46.9

strength in 1950, an off-year election under a Democratic administration. In 1952, each county illustrates the impact of Eisenhower on people's voting habits, even Dane County going Republican for congressman. The 1954 election again illustrates the general proposition that the presidential party loses votes in off-year elections. Without the influence of Eisenhower on the ticket, things got back closer to "normal" (this influence of "presidential coattails" will be discussed further in the next chapter). The election in 1956 again shows the influence of Eisenhower, three of the five counties showing decreases in Democratic strength. The year 1958 again illustrates the proposition shown in 1954 and 1950 (that the presidential party loses votes in off-year elections), and 1960 again shows a "normal" Democratic vote (Kennedy did not help the ticket—in fact, Kastenmeier, as did other Democrats, ran ahead of Kennedy in each of the counties—more of this in the next chapter).

But more to the point, each county shows an increase in Democratic strength over the twelve years. Dane county, which was already highly urban, reached 63.1 per cent Democratic in 1960. Waukesha, the county showing the greatest increase in population and the greatest increase in urban population, increased its Democratic percentage to 46.5. The Spearman Rank Order Correlation Coefficient between per cent urban increase and per cent Democratic increase between 1948 and 1960 is .30. That is, there is a relationship between how much each county increased in percentage urban population during these twelve years and how much they increased their Democratic vote. Eliminating Dane County because it was so highly urban and Democratic to begin with, the correlation for the other four counties becomes .80. The Spearman Rank Order Correlation Coefficient between per cent urban and per cent Democratic vote in 1960 is .90. That is, the larger the urban population within the county, the larger the Democratic vote.

What is suggested is that this factor of increasing urban population within the Second Congressional District of Wisconsin is working to the advantage of the Democratic party and its candidates. We are proceeding, in this analysis, under two well-substantiated generalizations which were discussed in Chapter 2. Outside of the South: (1) The larger the percentage urban population, the larger the percentage Democratic vote; and (2) as percentage urban increases, percentage Democratic vote increases. The Spearman Rank Order Correlations just reported provide the data for these two generalizations for the Second District. It now appears that the Second District of Wisconsin is sufficiently urban to insure a Democratic vote of over 50 per cent. But it is possible that some events may intervene to upset the Democratic-Republican ratio. These possible events may be listed as follows:

1. An unusually attractive Republican candidate for congressman; someone who, because of his personal appeal, is able to attract the votes of normally Democratic voters;

2. An unusually attractive Republican candidate for President in elections in presidential years, a candidate who is able to persuade large numbers of new or normally Democratic voters to vote a straight Republican ticket;

3. Some moral issue against the Democratic candidate (such as corruption), or some issue which will attract Democratic voters to the Republican candidate;

4. Low turnout among the normally Democratic voters.

With regard to the 1962 election, the Republican candidate is not "unusually" attractive, there is no presidential race (which may actually help Kastenmeier since Kennedy may actually have hurt the ticket in 1960), and Representative Kastenmeier is unlikely to come under fire for some offense which will hurt him (although the Republicans are trying with the "soft on communism" theme). And, as we have previously noted, both candidates will campaign vigorously, so that voting turnout should be at least "normal" for off-year elections.

There is one other contingency which we have to take up. It might be possible that Kastenmeier is winning in the Second District because he, in fact, acts like a Republican in his votes in Congress and hence is attracting many Republican voters to support him. This argument assumes that voters know Kastenmeier and know his stands on issues (the latter more unlikely than the former), and so is dubious to begin with. But a look at Kastenmeier's voting record in Congress should dispel any lingering doubts. *The Congressional Quarterly* lists the voting records of all congressmen on fifty domestic issues for the First Session of the Eighty-seventh Congress. These are roll-call votes on bills President Kennedy personally supported. A high support score indicates strong support for the President's program; a low support score indicates weak support for the President's program. Kastenmeier's support score for these fifty measures was 94 per cent. The average House Democratic support score was 73 per cent; the average GOP support score was 32 per cent. Certainly one cannot say that Kastenmeier is hobnobbing with the Republicans.[8]

We can conclude, then, that because the Second District of Wisconsin has more Democratic voters than Republican voters,

[8] *Congressional Quarterly Weekly Report,* No. 45, 1961.

because the candidates are relatively equal in resources, and because of the absence of personality or issue factors which might upset the prevalent Democratic-Republican ratio, Representative Kastenmeier should win in 1962. We can also conclude that what happens in the campaign will have little effect on the outcome. This is not to say that campaigns are unimportant. Their major function, however, is not to help people make up their minds whom to vote for, but rather to reinforce the party faithful and activate the latent followers. One of the ways in which Kastenmeier can lose would be from a low Democratic turnout. However, given a normal amount of campaigning by both candidates, Congressman Kastenmeier seems assured of re-election in 1962.

Summary and Conclusions

Election campaigns take place within a definite setting. It is the thesis of this chapter that there is little a candidate for public office can do that will affect the outcome of an election. Candidates, however, can attempt to manipulate the setting. If the candidate comes from a competitive district and/or if he has greater resources than his opponent, his chances of success in manipulating the outcome of the election will be greater. Generally, the strategy of the candidate whose party is behind is to attempt to manipulate personality and issue factors. The strategy of the candidate of the majority party is to stress party identification. Given normal issues and personalities, the strategy of the majority candidate should prevail.

On November 6, 1962, the voters in the Second Congressional District of Wisconsin went to the polls and re-elected Bob Kastenmeier by 52.4 per cent of the vote. This outcome lends some credence to the theory propounded in this chapter. It also seems that this kind of analysis lends itself to comparisons with other districts. Such comparative research would go far to validate, modify, or reject the basic proposition suggested here—that is, that congressional candidates have relatively little control over election outcomes. Comparative research should also help to specify, more clearly than here indicated, the kinds of conditions under which the generalization is true or false. For example, what kinds of candidates are likely to disturb the usual party ratio? What kinds of issues successfully overturn the party balance? Each of these questions has not only theoretical import, but practical significance as well. The ability of scholars to help politicians in campaigns could certainly be one important by-product of such research. Although it appears that the minority party candidate is almost always faced with an uphill fight, some campaign strategies and tactics may be better than others ("better" in terms of leading to electoral success). To isolate these strategies and tactics would be a most useful enterprise indeed.

5

An Explanation of Party Victories
In Mid-Term Elections

Introduction

There were a number of surprises in the 1962 mid-term elections. One could tick them off almost endlessly: former Vice President Nixon lost to Governor Brown in California; Wisconsin elected Democrats to the governorship and United States Senate (Reynolds and Nelson respectively) over heavily favored Republican opponents; both New Hampshire and Vermont elected Democratic governors; Oklahoma elected a Republican governor; Lister Hill, the incumbent Democratic senator from Alabama, retained his seat by only 50.8 per cent of the vote, and so on.

Perhaps the biggest surprise, however, was the showing that the Democratic party made in the Congress of the United States. We are all familiar with the general proposition that the party of the President loses seats in Congress in mid-term elections. Only once in the last sixty years has this generalization not been true. That was in 1934, during President Roosevelt's first term, when the Democratic party gained nine additional seats in the House of Representatives and ten additional seats in the Senate.

In 1962, a mid-term election under a Democratic President, an election in which the Republicans could be expected to gain seats, the Democratic party almost succeeded in repeating its performance of 1934. In the House of Representatives, the Republican party was expected to pick up from twelve to twenty-five seats. Instead, the Republicans gained two seats (increasing their number from 174 to 176). And, if one looks closely at these figures, the reason for any Republican gain at all in the House may be attributed to the party's unexpected showing in the southern and border states where six new Republicans were elected. In the northern and western states, the Republicans actually lost four seats. In the Senate, the sixty-four to thirty-six Democratic margin was expected to remain about the same. Instead, the Democrats gained four seats.[1]

We have two tasks before us in this chapter. The first is to explain why, in general, the President's party loses seats in Congress in mid-term elections. The second task is to explain why 1962 was an exception to this general rule.

Presidential Coattails and Mid-Term Elections

Let us start first with a general comment about the likelihood of party changes in Congress. The major point to be made is that most of the seats in Congress are "safe" for one party or the other. Using the House of Representatives as our illustration, we find that for the 434 of 437 congressional districts for which there are data,[2] only 94, or 22 per cent have had representatives from both parties during the period 1952 to 1962. Fully 51 per cent (222) have gone to one party and have never had an election in the last ten years in which the winner received less than 55 per cent of the vote. For the 1962 election, the *New York*

---

[1] Before the 1963 session got under way, two Democratic senators died, Chavez of New Mexico and Kerr of Oklahoma. In each case, the governor of the state resigned and was appointed by the succeeding governor (the former lt. governor) to the vacant office. In New Mexico, the governor was a Republican, and in Oklahoma, a Democrat. Hence, although after the 1962 election the party make-up of the Senate was sixty-eight to thirty-two in favor of the Democrats, it is now sixty-seven to thirty-three.

[2] Because of the admission of Alaska and Hawaii into the Union, the membership of the House of Representatives was temporarily increased to 437 members. Three of the 437 districts (Alaska, Hawaii, and one district in the state of Washington) did not have data for the five elections.

Times reported that only eighty-seven seats were marginal seats in 1962 (that is, because they were won by under 55 per cent of the vote in 1960, they were the most likely to change party hands in 1962).[3] The *Congressional Quarterly*, on the basis of additional criteria, listed forty seats as "doubtful," with forty-four as "leaning" to one party or the other. It listed 194 as safe Democratic, and 117 as safe Republican.[4]

What these figures mean is that from 75 to 80 per cent of the House seats are usually not even in question in any given election. If a party is going to pick up seats, it will have to do so by winning a large proportion of the few relatively competitive congressional districts. The Republicans, for example, really had no chance of winning a majority in the House of Representatives in 1962. Even if the Republicans won all eighty-seven of the districts listed as "marginal" by the *New York Times*, it would still leave the House with 223 Democrats and 212 Republicans. Even to pick up seats (let alone win a majority), the Republicans would have to keep most or all of their own forty-eight marginal seats, and win some of the twenty-nine marginal Democratic seats.

We can see, then, that to pick up seats in an election is a difficult task and involves elections in a relatively few marginal or closely competitive districts. Although all 435 House seats are up for election every two years, only a relatively small number of them could change party hands. With this limitation of the number of potential seats which can change party hands in mind, we can now begin to explain why it is that, under "normal" circumstances, the President's party loses seats in mid-term elections.

In presidential elections, approximately 60 per cent of the eligible voters go to the polls. In mid-term congressional elections the percentage drops off to approximately 45 per cent. This differential of 15 per cent consists mostly of "unstable" voters, people who do not have strong party identifications, who have no lasting interest in politics, who are not terribly knowledgeable about politics, and who have little concern with the

[3] *New York Times*, "News of the Week in Review," Sunday, July 29, 1962.
[4] Congressional Quarterly Special Report, Elections of 1962, Part II of

outcome of the election.[5] They are people who are motivated to vote in presidential elections but not in mid-term elections because of the excitement and additional stimuli which are present in the former but not in the latter. Furthermore, and this is the crucial point, these unstable voters are likely, in presidential elections, to cast their lot with the most exciting presidential candidate or in favor of the presidential candidate with the most significant issue.[6] This additional number of unstable voters is likely to vote disproportionately in favor of one candidate. It is not true, for example, that the Democratic candidate always benefits by high voting turnout.[7] The party with the most exciting candidate or issues will benefit, whether it is the Democratic or the Republican. During the 1930's and 1940's the unstable voters came out to support Roosevelt; during the 1950's they came out for Eisenhower.

In addition, many of these unstable voters who are likely to vote in elections in presidential years but not in mid-term elections, although less likely to vote the straight party ticket than strong party identifiers, will cast a straight party ballot for the other members of the presidential candidate's party, especially at the national level. If they split their tickets at all, it is much more likely to be for state and local offices than for other national offices.[8] Being neither very knowledgeable about the other candidates, nor motivated to vote for political offices other than for President, they have little reason to split their tickets.

The unstable voters, because of their higher turnout in presidential elections, contribute disproportionately to the winning presidential candidate's margin of victory. Also, because many of these unstable voters vote a straight party ticket, especially at the national level, many of the congressional candidates of the President's party receive additional votes in presidential elections which they would not receive in mid-term elections. As we

[5] Angus Campbell, Gerald Gurin, and Warren E. Miller, *The Voter Decides* (Evanston, Ill.: Row, Peterson, 1954); and Angus Campbell, Philip E. Converse, Warren E. Miller, and Donald E. Stokes, *The American Voter* (New York: Wiley, 1960).

[6] See William A. Glaser, "Fluctuations in Turnout," in William N. McPhee and William A. Glaser, eds., *Public Opinion and Congressional Elections* (New York: Free Press of Glencoe, 1962), pp. 19–52.

[7] See Angus Campbell *et al.*, *The American Voter, op. cit.*, chap. v.

[8] Angus Campbell *et al.*, *The Voter Decides, op. cit.*, chap. ii.

Congressional Quarterly Weekly Report No. 18, 1962.

mentioned earlier, the seats which are likely to change party hands in any given election are those which are marginal for either party, that is, districts in which the two-party vote is relatively close. For some congressional candidates, the additional votes are enough to provide them with their needed margin of victory. They are, in this sense, swept into office on the President's "coattails." When the attractive candidate or issues favor the Democrats, additional Democrats win seats in Congress. When the factors of candidate appeal or issues favor the Republicans (as they did during Eisenhower's eight years), additional Republicans win office.

Now we can easily see what happens in mid-term elections. The unstable voters are less likely to vote because of the lack of a presidential race, and the President's party is likely to lose many of the seats that it picked up on the President's coattails in the preceding presidential election. Hence, the general rule: the President's party loses seats in Congress in mid-term elections.

The 1962 Mid-Term Election

We can now turn to the second question to be answered in this chapter: How does one explain the narrow Republican gain of two seats in the House of Representatives (a loss of four seats in the North), and a loss of four seats in the Senate in 1962? This was a mid-term election and the President is a Democrat. The Republicans should have picked up seats in the Senate, and they were expected to do much better than they did in the northern House districts.

To answer this question we need not resort to ad hoc explanations. That is, some interpreters of the 1962 Democratic victory suggested that the reason lay in President Kennedy's high personal popularity as reflected in the Gallup polls, or that the American people are becoming more liberal, or that the Democratic victory was a sign of support for the President in the Cuban crisis. Rather, the explanation of the Democratic success in 1962 may be handled perfectly well by the factors examined above, and we need not rely on assumptions about the President's popularity, liberal-conservative issues, or foreign policy. Actually, if issues were important at all in 1962, they favored

Republicans in the South who attacked Democratic candidates as being too liberal, especially on race issues.

To answer the question of why the Democrats fared so well in 1962, we need to remember the conditions under which the generalization that the President's party loses seats in mid-term elections is true. It is true when there is a presidential candidate or issue which disproportionately attracts unstable voters to vote for the presidential candidate and other national candidates of his party.

Going back to the 1960 presidential election, was there a presidential coattail effect? Did the Democratic winner gain most of the unstable vote and sweep into office with him a number of Democratic congressmen? The answer to both of these questions is a resounding no. Kennedy did not seem more attractive, personally, than did Nixon to most voters. The major issue in 1960 was not candidate appeal, but rather religion. Because of the religious issue, many of the unstable voters were voting pro- and anti-Catholic. This unstable vote split about evenly for and against the two candidates. As a matter of fact, the best estimate of the effect of the religious issue in 1960 is that it cost Kennedy about one and one-half million votes.[9]

Two other facts also lead to the conclusion that President Kennedy did not create a coattail effect in the 1960 election. President Kennedy's winning electoral margin was a little over one hundred thousand votes. This contrasts with a high of 11 million for Roosevelt, and 9.5 million for Eisenhower. Kennedy certainly did not demonstrate his superior vote-drawing power in 1960. Given the fact that there are about three people in the United States who identify with the Democratic party for every two who identify with the Republican party,[10] Kennedy's one hundred-thousand-vote margin makes it look as if Nixon was the candidate who drew disproportionately from the unstable voters.

Further, the Democratic party actually lost twenty seats in the House of Representatives and two seats in the Senate in

[9] See Philip E. Converse, Angus Campbell, Warren E. Miller, Donald E. Stokes, "Stability and Change in 1960: A Reinstating Election," *American Political Science Review*, LV (June, 1961), 269–81.

[10] Angus Campbell *et al.*, *The Voter Decides, op. cit.*; and Angus Campbell *et al.*, *The American Voter, op. cit.*

1960, an unusual occurrence. Usually, the President's party picks up seats in presidential election years. And, President Kennedy actually ran behind the Democratic canidates in 331 congressional districts. In 226 districts, Kennedy ran behind by 5 percentage points or more.[11] This is additional evidence that Kennedy was not pulling the ticket with him.

The absence of a positive coattail effect in 1960 leads to the conclusion that the usual result in mid-term elections—that is, that the President's party should lose seats in 1962—would not occur. Because the reasons were not present for a loss of Democratic seats in 1962, the loss did not occur. Only because of the increased strength of the Republican party in the South did the Republicans gain two seats in the House, and the Democrats picked up four seats in the Senate.

Conclusion

This analysis illustrates the need to be very cautious in merely extrapolating past findings into the future. That is, merely because the President's party has lost seats in mid-term elections (with one exception) for the last sixty years does not mean that it will happen next time. We must be careful to explore the underlying reasons why the findings are what they are in order to see if the conditions under which the findings are true are present or absent. If the conditions are present, we may be relatively confident that the generalization will hold true. If the conditions are not present, we must not expect the usual result to occur.

[11] *Congressional Quarterly Weekly Report*, No. 15, 1961.

Part II

CONSTITUENCY INFLUENCES ON CONGRESSMEN

6

Why the Senate Is More Liberal
Than the House

Part II of this book will be concerned with the relationship between various constituency influences and their effects on congressional decision-making.

In Part I we saw that a knowledge of social, economic, and
political factors within constituencies helps us to explain differential rates of participation in elections by citizens, how voting
participation varies by party and section of the country, and
how such participation, or lack of it, affects other aspects of the
political system (stability-instability, campaign strategies and
tactics, electoral success of candidates, and party fortunes in
mid-term as opposed to presidential elections). Part II will concentrate on the importance of social, economic, and political factors within congressional constituencies in the determination of
governmental policy. It is hoped that such an analysis will lead
to a broader understanding of the relationships between constituents, their representatives, and public-policy—relationships so
necessary for the functioning of democratic governments.

Introduction

This chapter will deal with how the manner in which members
of representative institutions are elected and the kinds of constituencies of which the institutions are composed can affect the

type of public policy which is likely to flow from those institutions. That is, electoral systems, as well as many other procedural rules, are not neutral in their impact on the course of public policy. For example, we are all familiar with the argument that the manner in which the President is elected has a significant influence on the public policies preferred by presidential candidates as opposed to the average congressional candidate of the same party. The operation of the Electoral College under the unit rule specifies that the winner of a plurality of votes in the state wins all of the electoral votes in that state. Because this unit rule in the Electoral College gives candidates an added bonus if they can win the states with large electoral votes, presidential candidates tend to overrepresent large, urban, two-party states, and minority groups within these states.[1] This is an example of how the procedural rules can affect the content of public policy proposals.

Similarly, we can expect that the fact that senators represent whole states while congressmen represent relatively smaller, more homogeneous districts within states might have some impact on the type of legislation preferred by the average member in each institution. We explore, in this chapter, how this difference in type of constituency represented affects the public policies which are likely to be produced within the Senate and House of Representatives.

The Intent and Consequences of a Bicameral Legislature

Commentators on American political history find that the compromise to establish a bicameral national legislature was expected to have the following consequences: (1) the upper house, or Senate, was to be more representative of the well-to-do, propertied classes in the United States, and (2) the lower house, or House of Representatives, was to be more attuned to "mass" pressure, especially from the debtor, unpropertied, lower classes. This, of course, was in addition to the large vs. small state contro-

---

[1] See Robert A. Dahl, *A Preface To Democratic Theory* (Chicago: University of Chicago Press, 1956), chaps. iv and v; and Lewis A. Froman, Jr., *People and Politics: An Analysis of the American Political System* (Englewood Cliffs, N.J.: Prentice-Hall, 1962), chap. vi.

versy which a bicameral legislature also helped to solve. Hence, state legislatures, not "the people," were to elect senators; only the members of the House were to be elected by the general population. The anticipated consequences of a bicameral legislature elected in this fashion were that the House would be a more liberal body, the Senate more conservative.

Recent observations of Congress seem to belie these expectations. Although systematic studies are lacking, current commentators point out that the Senate is more liberal than the House. Undoubtedly, changes in the method of electing senators, as well as the expansion of the franchise, have had a great deal of influence on the policy preferences of senators as well as congressmen. But these changes merely help to explain why there should be no differences between the Senate and the House. Both are now popularly elected by a system which allows for universal suffrage. Why should the Senate be more liberal than the House?

Two problems will occupy us in the next three sections: first, to answer the question, is the Senate more liberal than the House?, and second, to provide an explanation for the answer.

Is the Senate More Liberal Than the House?

Evidence for the proposition that the Senate is more liberal than the House will be presented in two different ways. First, we shall inspect all of the bills submitted to Congress by President Kennedy during the First Session of the Eighty-seventh Congress to ascertain how they fared in the hands of each house of Congress. Second, we shall examine, in much closer detail, ten of President Kennedy's most important requests for legislation to see how each bill was amended by the Senate and the House. The first measure will provide a comparison between the Senate and the House in the treatment of President Kennedy's legislative program. By making two assumptions, we can infer something about the liberalism of the Senate as compared with the House. The second measure will allow us to apply a much more rigorous definition of liberalism to a comparatively few bills in each house. The first measure has the advantage of breadth, the second of detail.

The *Congressional Quarterly Almanac* lists 355 pieces of legislation submitted by President Kennedy in the First Session of the Eighty-seventh Congress.[2] These 355 pieces of legislation represent specific requests for legislative action by President Kennedy. Of these 355, 10 were treaties. Since the House does not act on treaties, these have been excluded from the analysis. Also, of the twenty-nine tax bills (which must originate in the House), twenty-three did not get beyond the hearing stage in the House of Representatives. These twenty-three are not counted since there is no basis of comparison with what the Senate might have done. Our list of 355, then, is pared to 322.

These 322 bills were then scored by the *Congressional Quarterly Almanac* as to whether they were treated favorably or unfavorably by the committees in each house of Congress and, if they reached this stage, on the floor of each house of Congress. When modifications of the original requests occurred, the *Congressional Quarterly* evaluated the outcome to determine whether it was closer to approval or disapproval of the President's request. On the basis of the scores provided in the *Congressional Quarterly Almanac,* the number of favorable and unfavorable committee and floor actions in the House were totaled and compared with the number of favorable and unfavorable committee and floor actions in the Senate for the 322 pieces of legislation submitted by President Kennedy. It can be inferred that the body which has the greatest number of favorable actions, and least number of unfavorable actions, is more liberal. This inference follows from the tenable assumptions that President Kennedy is a liberal, and that the program which he submits to Congress is a liberal program. Table 6.1 presents the data on favorable and unfavorable committee and floor actions in the House and Senate.

The data in Table 6.1 support the hypothesis, as measured, that the Senate is more liberal than the House. In committees and on the floor, the Senate acted favorably on a larger percentage of Kennedy's proposals, and unfavorably on a smaller percentage, than did the House. In the committee stage, the Senate acted favorably on 207 (64.3 per cent) and unfavorably on 44 (13.6 per cent) pieces of legislation compared with 192 (59.6 per cent) and 56 (17.4 per cent) respectively in the House. Simi-

[2] (Washington, D.C.: Congressional Quarterly, Inc.), XVII, 91–103.

TABLE 6.1

Favorable and Unfavorable Committee and Floor Actions in the House
and Senate on 322 Pieces of Legislation Submitted by President
Kennedy, 87th Congress, 1st Session*

House of Congress	Actions on Kennedy Legislation											
	Committee						Floor					
	Favorable		Unfavorable		No Action		Favorable		Unfavorable		No Action	
	N	%	N	%	N	%	N	%	N	%	N	%
House	192	(59.6)	56	(17.4)	74	(23.0)	166	(51.5)	66	(20.5)	90	(28.0)
Senate	207	(64.3)	44	(13.6)	71	(22.1)	185	(57.4)	51	(15.8)	86	(26.8)

*Data from the *Congressional Quarterly Almanac* (Washington, D.C.: Congressional Quarterly, Inc., 1951), Vol. XVII.

larly, in floor action, the Senate acted favorably on 185 (57.4 per cent) and unfavorably on 51 (15.8 per cent) of Kennedy's proposals, the House, 166 (51.5 per cent) and 66 (20.5 per cent), respectively. Although the differences are not large, each of the comparisons supports the hypothesis. Additional confirmation is also supplied by the slight differences found in the "No Action" columns. If Kennedy's program is considered liberal, and if the Senate is more liberal than the House, we would expect greater inaction on the part of the House as compared with the Senate. Table 6.1 confirms this additional deduction.

The above data, however, must be used cautiously. Certainly it is not being argued here that all of the 322 pieces of legislation submitted by President Kennedy may be classified on a liberal-conservative continuum. Hence, findings such as the above which may entail such an implication should be supplemented by other data. To provide a more detailed treatment of the question of which house of Congress is more liberal, ten Kennedy proposals were chosen for closer examination.

The *Congressional Quarterly Almanac* lists twenty-five bills as being the most important of Kennedy's requests facing the First Session of the Eighty-seventh Congress.[3] Eight of these twenty-five had to do with foreign affairs and reorganization of the executive branch and were eliminated. Of the remaining seventeen having to do with domestic welfare programs, ten were randomly sampled for more detailed analysis.

These ten proposals constitute the heart of President Kennedy's social welfare program, consisting of bills for education, civil rights, depressed areas, minimum wage, emergency feed grains, housing, social security, water pollution, unemployment, and aid to dependent children. Liberalism in the context of this section, then, will refer to social and economic domestic issues. An examination of the fate of each bill in the House and the Senate, and, where appropriate, a comparison of the House version of the bill with the Senate version of the bill before Conference Committee, should provide a more precise comparison of liberalism between the two houses of Congress.[4] No attempt, however, has been made to weight the different provisions in each bill.

[3] *Ibid.*
[4] Data from the *Congressional Quarterly Almanac, ibid.*

Two of the proposals are easily disposed of.

1. Aid to Education—passed by the Senate but rejected by the House. Senate considered more liberal.

2. Civil Rights Commission—by-passed committee hearings in the Senate for fear that the bill would never reach the floor. The House version was accepted on the floor of the Senate as an amendment to another bill. House considered more liberal.

The other eight issues require close inspection of the different versions before Conference Committee.

3. Depressed Areas—House bill before Conference Committee and Senate bill before Conference Committee similar except for two provisions in the House bill which were considered more liberal than Senate provisions (e.g., the House provided for 100 per cent of the cost of loans under the provisions of the bill, the Senate, 65 per cent), and five provisions in the Senate bill which were considered more liberal than House provisions (e.g., financing the $300 million lending authority by direct Treasury financing rather than congressional appropriations as provided in the House version). Senate considered more liberal.

4. Minimum Wage—House and Senate bills before Conference Committee similar except in the following respects: House—raised minimum wage for those already covered to $1.15; Senate—raised to $1.25 in two years and two stages. House—workers newly covered, 1,300,000; Senate, 4,086,000. House—minimum wage for newly covered workers, $1.00; Senate—$1.25 in four steps over three years. House—no overtime for newly covered workers; Senate—most newly covered workers provided with overtime pay. On all four differing provisions the Senate may be considered more liberal than the House.

5. Emergency Feed Grains—nine differing provisions between the Senate and House versions of the bill before Conference Committee, five of which were considered more liberal in favor of the House (e.g., the market-sales provision in the House bill allowed the Secretary of Agriculture to flood the market with surplus grain, thereby driving down the price of the grain and hurting those who do not participate in the program [those who do participate in the program receive price supports]); four of the provisions were considered more liberal in favor of the Senate version (e.g., up to one-half of funds to be paid to farmers who retire crops from acreage may be paid in advance; no com-

parable provision in the House bill). Overall, House considered more liberal than the Senate.

6. Omnibus Housing—ten provisions in the House bill before Conference Committee considered to be more liberal (e.g., $100 million increase in direct loan fund for housing for elderly as compared with $50 million provided by the Senate), and nine provisions in the Senate bill before Conference Committee were considered to be more liberal (e.g., $80 million increase in urban planning grants as compared with $30 million provided by the House). The House bill also authorized more total funds for the housing program than did the Senate bill. House considered more liberal than the Senate.

7. Social Security—identical bills passed by the Senate and House before Conference Committee except for two liberalizing provisions in the Senate bill (increased ceiling on earnings, and temporary assistance for United States nationals returning home in distressed circumstances). Senate considered more liberal.

8. Water Pollution—House bill before Conference Committee contained three provisions considered more liberal than the Senate version (e.g., the House extended the administration's abatement plan for ten years, the Senate for five years), and the Senate bill contained two provisions considered more liberal than the House version (e.g., $25 million for research into new methods of sewage treatment). Overall, the House bill considered more liberal than the Senate.

9. Temporary Unemployment Benefits—four major differences between the House and Senate versions before Conference Committee, two increasing the liberalism of the House version (e.g., the Senate provided for reduced benefits to persons receiving pensions, the House did not), and two increasing the liberalism of the Senate version (e.g., the Senate provided a clause to increase the ceiling on federal grants, the House did not). Neither Senate nor House considered more liberal.

10. Aid to Dependent Children—the Senate added nine amendments to the House bill, five of them liberalizing the bill (e.g., increasing from 80 to 100 per cent the federal share of costs of grants to states to train public welfare personnel), three of them reducing the liberal benefits provided by the House (e.g., postponed date for the Department of Health, Education,

and Welfare's order cutting off federal funds from states that denied relief to children from "unsuitable" homes), and one indeterminate. Senate considered more liberal than the House.

Several interesting findings accrue from the above analysis. First, the Senate is by no means more liberal than the House on all bills. On certain issues, the House was considered more liberal than the Senate (civil rights, emergency feed grains, housing, and water pollution). Second, even on bills in which the Senate or the House, overall, was considered more liberal, the other house usually had several amendments which were more liberal. In summary, however, on the ten bills above, the Senate was considered to be more liberal on five, the House more liberal on four, and one indeterminate. Of the fifty-eight differing provisions in the eight bills which reached the Conference Committee, thirty-three, or 57 per cent, were liberalizing Senate amendments. Again the evidence, although by a narrow margin, indicates that the Senate is a more liberal body than the House. This detailed examination of ten important bills, together with the earlier data on Kennedy's total program, presents convincing evidence that the Senate is at least slightly more liberal than is the House.

Why the Senate Is More Liberal Than the House

Two reasons are usually given for the fact that the Senate is likely to pass, on the whole, more liberal legislation than is the House. The first has to do with the manner in which the two houses are organized, the second with the kinds of constituencies the members of each house represent.

As to the first reason, the proposition that the Senate is more liberal than the House is supported in the following manner. The seniority rule in each house of Congress specifies that the committee members of the majority and minority parties who have been on the committee for the longest periods of continuous service are the chairman and the ranking minority member, respectively, of that committee. Also, important committee assignments and other leadership positions often go to members of each house who either have long periods of service or who can demonstrate that they are in no danger of being defeated at the polls.[5] Those members from less competitive districts, who are better able to gain seniority, are also more likely to come from districts with constituency characteristics more favorable to a conservative rather than a liberal position on many issues.[6]

Further, when the Democrats are in control of each house, southern members of the party, who tend to be less liberal than northern members,[7] have a disproportionate number of leadership positions. For example, in the Eighty-seventh Congress, although southern members represent only about 25 per cent of the total membership in each house, they chair, in each house, over 50 per cent of the committees. This disproportionate influence of the more conservative members in each house means that liberal positions supported by other members of Congress are not likely to prevail.

However, since the House of Representatives is considered, by most observers, to be more hierarchically organized than is the Senate (that is, leaders in the House have more power vis-à-vis other members than do Senate leaders),[8] the fact that leaders are more conservative makes a bigger difference in the House than in the Senate. Given the more hierarchical power structure in the House, the positions supported by the more liberal non-leaders are even less likely to prevail than they are in the Senate. For these reasons, then, the public policies passed by the House will be more conservative than those passed by the Senate.

Although evidence for most of the above argument is fairly well established,[9] the weak link in the chain of the argument

[5] With regard to committee assignments to the House Appropriations Committee, see Richard F. Fenno, Jr., "The House Appropriations Committee as a Political System: The Problem of Integration," *American Political Science Review*, LVI (June, 1962), 310–24.

For committees in general, see Nicholas A. Masters, "House Committee Assignments, *American Political Science Review*, LV (June, 1961), 345–58. For a discussion of the seniority rule, see George Goodwin, Jr., "The Seniority System in Congress," *American Political Science Review*, LIII (June, 1959), 412–37.

[6] See Chapter 9 for evidence supporting this proposition.

[7] See Chapter 7.

[8] See William H. Riker, *Democracy in the United States* (New York: Macmillan, 1953), chap. v.

[9] Goodwin, *op. cit.;* Fenno, *op. cit.;* Lester W. Jackson, *District Safety, Seniority, and Chairmanships in the House of Representatives* (Unpublished Master's thesis, University of Wisconsin, 1961); and Chapters 7 and 9 of this book.

comes in the differences in liberalism-conservatism between leaders and non-leaders. Others report that there is little, or only slight evidence to indicate that the leaders of either house are more conservative than the rank-and-file.[10] As a further test of the hypothesis, representatives of the Eighty-seventh Congress, First Session were divided into leaders and non-leaders.[11] As a measure of liberalism in voting, the Larger Federal Role Support Score from the *Congressional Quarterly* was used.[12] As a measure of conservatism in voting, the Conservative Coalition Support Score from the *Congressional Quarterly* was used.[13] Table 6.2 indicates that for Democrats, at least, the hypothesis is confirmed. Although the differences are relatively small, leaders of the Democratic party in the House do have a smaller average liberalism score and a higher average conservatism score than do non-leaders. (For the Republicans, the difference between leaders and non-leaders on the liberalism score is exceedingly small, and is in the wrong direction on the conservatism score.)[14]

The argument, then, that the House is more conservative than the Senate because of conservative leadership and greater hier-

[10] See Duncan MacRae, Jr., *Dimensions Of Congressional Voting* ("University of California Publication in Sociology and Social Institutions" [Berkeley: University of California Press, 1958]), I, 203–390, esp. pp. 289–98; David B. Truman, *The Congressional Party* (New York: Wiley, 1959), esp. chaps. iv and vi; and Goodwin, *op. cit.* Although Goodwin has no evidence on differences in liberalism between leaders and non-leaders, he does have data on party unity which indicate little difference between leaders and rank-and-file on party unity scores.

[11] Leaders include the majority leader and whip along with the twenty-one standing committee chairmen for the Democrats, and the minority leader and whip and twenty-one ranking minority members on the standing committees for the Republicans. Although the Speaker is also a party leader, he rarely votes. Hence, he is excluded from this analysis.

[12] See the *Congressional Quarterly Weekly Report*, No. 42, 1961, pp. 1751–63. The Larger Federal Role Index consists of ten House roll calls offering congressmen a choice between a larger or smaller federal role on various domestic issues.

[13] See *ibid.*, No. 44, 1961, pp. 1796–1806. The Conservative Coalition Support Index consists of twenty-three roll calls on which a majority of southern Democrats joined with a majority of Republicans in opposition to a majority of northern Democrats.

[14] Assuming this variable of leader, non-leader differences in liberalism-conservatism to be important in explaining differences in liberalism between the two houses, this may indicate that perhaps when the Republicans are in power, the Senate and the House will be more nearly equal in liberalism. This points up the need for comparative research on a number of Congresses.

TABLE 6.2

Liberalism and Conservatism Scores of Leaders and Non-Leaders in the House of Representatives, 87th Congress, 1st Session*

Members by Party	Average Scores†	
	Larger Federal Role	*Conservative Coalition Support*
Democrats		
Leaders	6.74	3.48
Non-Leaders	7.45	2.84
Republicans		
Leaders	1.20	6.65
Non-Leaders	1.24	6.95

*Data from the *Congressional Quarterly Weekly Report*, Nos. 42 and 44, 1961.

† Scales may vary from 0 to 9. Higher scores under Larger Federal Role indicate a greater degree of liberalism. Higher scores under Conservative Coalition Support indicate a greater degree of conservatism.

archical organization seems to be at least partially true, but the differences in liberalism-conservatism between leaders and non-leaders are so small that the question warrants investigation of additional explanations.

Constituency Differences as a Second Explanation

The second reason to be advanced in this chapter to explain why the Senate is more liberal than the House has to do with the nature of the constituencies which senators and congressmen represent. Senators, whose constituencies are entire states, are faced, on the whole, with more heterogeneous electorates than are congressmen, whose constituencies are smaller and likely to be more homogeneous. This is most obviously true for each state taken separately. The senators from that state have the entire state as their constituencies, congressmen only a portion of it (except for the eight states whose congressmen are elected at large).

The second explanation, then, for why the Senate is more liberal than the House will have two parts. First, we will show that certain population characteristics of congressional districts are associated with liberal and conservative voting records of congressmen.[15] We will then show that there are more House districts below than above the state average on population characteristics

[15] This point will be explored further in the next chapter.

which are associated with liberalism, and more House districts above than below the state average on population characteristics which are associated with conservatism. Since the senators' constituencies are the state averages, if there are more congressional districts below the state averages on characteristics associated with liberalism and more congressional districts above the state averages on characteristics associated with conservatism, this will be evidence that one reason why the Senate is more liberal than the House has to do with the nature of the constituencies which senators and congressmen represent. Senators are more liberal because, on the whole, their constituencies have more of the characteristics associated with liberalism than do congressmen's constituencies.

The three population characteristics chosen for this study are (1) race (per cent non-white), (2) residence (per cent urban), and (3) socioeconomic status (per cent owner-occupied dwelling units).[16] Table 6.3 relates these population characteristics with voting in Congress. Congressmen from those districts which are below the state averages for percentage non-white and percentage urban were predicted to be less liberal than those congressmen from districts above the state averages for these two characteristics. Similarly, congressmen from those districts which are above the state averages for percentage owner-occupied dwelling units were also predicted to be less liberal. These hypotheses are fully consistent with the literature relating population characteristics with liberalism and conservatism. Nonwhite, urban, and lower socioeconomic groups are more likely to be liberal than their opposites (white, rural, and higher socioeconomic status groups).[17]

[16] Data for per cent non-white and per cent owner-occupied dwelling units come from the *Congressional District Data Book, Districts of the 87th Congress* (U.S. Department of Commerce, Bureau of the Census [Washington, D.C.: Government Printing Office, 1961]). Data for per cent urban come from the *Congressional Quarterly Weekly Report*, No. 8, 1962. The definition of urban area is that of the Bureau of the Census, 1960.

[17] See, for example, Seymour M. Lipset, Paul F. Lazarsfeld, Allen H. Barton, and Juan Linz, "The Psychology of Voting: An Analysis of Political Behavior," in Gardner Lindzey, ed., *Handbook of Social Psychology* (Cambridge, Mass.: Addison-Wesley, 1954), pp. 1124–77; Bernard Berelson, Paul F. Lazarsfeld, and William N. McPhee, *Voting* (Chicago: University of Chicago Press, 1954); and Angus Campbell, Philip E. Converse, Warren E. Miller, and Donald E. Stokes, *The American Voter* (New York: Wiley, 1960).

TABLE 6.3

Liberalism Scores for Congressmen Who Come from Districts Above and Below State Averages on Three Population Characteristics*

| Population Characteristics | Mean Average Scores† Congressional Districts | | | |
	Above State Average	N	*Below* State Average	N
Per Cent Non-White	6.22	(155)	4.14	(264)
Per Cent Urban	5.52	(191)	4.44	(232)
Per Cent Owner-Occupied Dwelling Units	4.07	(248)	6.16	(175)

*Data compiled from the *Congressional District Data Book, Districts of the 87th Congress* (U.S. Department of Commerce, Bureau of the Census [Washington, D.C.: Government Printing Office, 1961]), *Congressional Quarterly Weekly Report*, No. 8, 1962, and the *Congressional Quarterly Weekly Report*, No. 42, 1961.

† Liberalism averages are based on the Larger Federal Role Index. Mean averages may vary from 0 to 9, a larger average denoting a higher degree of liberalism.

Table 6.3 illustrates that congressmen who come from districts below the state averages on percentage non-white and percentage urban, and above the state averages on percentage owner-occupied dwelling units are less liberal than their opposites.

Table 6.3 also illustrates that there are more congressional districts which are below the state averages on characteristics associated with liberalism than above the state averages, and more House districts above the state averages on population characteristics associated with conservatism than below the state averages. There are more districts below the state averages for percentage non-white than above (264 to 155), more districts below the state averages on percentage urban than above (232 to 191), and more districts above the state averages for percentage owner-occupied units than below (248 to 175). Since the state averages are the senators' districts, and there are more House districts below the state averages on population characteristics associated with liberalism than above the state averages, and more House districts above the state averages on population characteristics associated with conservatism than below the state averages, we may conclude that this difference in the kinds of constituencies which are represented in the two houses provides additional explanation of why the Senate is more liberal than the House.

Summary and Conclusions

We have been concerned, in this chapter, with a dual question: Is the Senate more liberal than the House of Representatives, and, if so, why? We presented two sets of data to support the proposition that the Senate is more liberal than the House. The first set analyzed the fate of 322 bills personally supported by President Kennedy. We found that Senate committee and floor action was more likely to be favorable and less likely to be unfavorable than House committee and floor action in the handling of these bills. Assuming that President Kennedy is a liberal and that the legislative program he submits to Congress will, by and large, be a liberal program, this data was considered evidence that the Senate is more liberal than the House.

The second set of data concerned ten of President Kennedy's most important requests for domestic welfare legislation. We found that the Senate versions of these bills before Conference Committee were, on the whole, more likely than the House versions to be liberal in orientation. This more detailed examination using more elaborate criteria of liberalism-conservatism provided additional evidence that the Senate is more liberal than the House.

In answering the question of why the Senate is more liberal than the House, we found two explanations to be useful. The first had to do with structural reasons, the second with the kinds of constituencies which senators and representatives tend to represent. We found leaders to be slightly more conservative than non-leaders, and this fact, coupled with the hypothesis that the House is more hierarchically organized than the Senate, provides one explanation. Given the differences in organization between the two houses, and the differences in policy preferences between leaders and non-leaders, these organizational differences help us to explain why the Senate is more likely to support liberal legislation than is the House.

The second reason why the Senate is more liberal than the House concerned the differences in constituencies represented in each house. We found that there are more House districts below state averages on population characteristics associated with liberalism than above state averages (percentage non-white and percentage urban), and more House districts above state averages on population characteristics associated with conservatism than below state averages (percentage owner-occupied dwelling units). Since the senators' districts are the state averages, these data provided an additional explanation of why the Senate is more liberal than the House. Not only does the manner in which the houses are organized make a difference, but also the kinds of constituencies which are represented in each house. Both institutional factors and factors exogenous to the institution were helpful in our explanation.

7

Constituency Differences Between Parties
and Congressional Roll-Call Voting*

In the next three chapters, we will be concerned with various factors as they influence the voting of congressmen. Chapter 7 will deal with four social and economic variables within constituencies, party differences, and votes by congressmen on a number of important political issues. The major question to be asked is: How do differences in environmental circumstances among constituencies affect the way in which congressmen vote? Chapter 8 will deal with the importance of the particular Democrat or Republican holding office. That is, does the man himself, apart from his party and constituency, have some impact on public policy questions? In Chapter 9 we will be concerned with the effect of competitiveness of districts on roll-call voting. Does the fact that some congressmen are in greater danger of losing office than others by virtue of the fact that they come from competitive districts affect their voting in Congress? Answers to

* This chapter is a revised and enlarged version of an earlier paper, "Inter-Party Constituency Differences and Congressional Voting Behavior," *American Political Science Review*, LVII (March, 1963), 57–61. I would like to thank the *American Political Science Review* for permission to use much of the body of that paper.

each of these questions are of crucial importance to an understanding of representative government.

Introduction

This chapter will deal with the relationships among constituency factors, party differences, and congressional voting. This interest follows from a prior concern with one of the most important problems in democratic government, to wit, the relationship between the preferences of the governed and the outcomes of governmental processes. In democratic governments, we would expect to find some degree of relationship between how representatives of the people act on matters of public policy and the kinds of people who are being represented. Studies of legislatures provide fertile field for such explorations, since legislators usually represent different, relatively small segments of the population.

An argument is not being made here that the way congressmen vote on bills on the floor of Congress is the only factor which determines the course of public policy. Besides the obvious fact that the President, executive agencies, and the courts must also be taken into account in any complete examination of the policy-making process, exclusive reliance on roll-call voting by legislators ignores the influence of other important legislative processes. Many bills introduced in Congress, for example, never reach the floor for a vote. Of President Kennedy's 355 legislative requests in 1961, less than half reached the floor of both houses for a vote.[1] Or, more generally, of the 3,071 bills and resolutions introduced in the Senate in the First Session of the Eighty-seventh Congress, about one-third, or 1,133 were passed. In the House of Representatives, which does not allow multiple sponsorship of the same bill (and hence encourages many members to sponsor identical bills), 10,955 bills and resolutions introduced in 1961 resulted in 1,234 being passed.[2]

Not only do considerably less than half of the total number of

[1] See the *Congressional Quarterly Almanac* (Washington, D.C.: Congressional Quarterly, Inc., 1961), Vol. XVII.

[2] Floyd M. Riddick, "The Eighty-seventh Congress: First Session," *Western Political Quarterly*, XV (June, 1962), 254–74.

bills and resolutions introduced in Congress reach the floor, but those that do make the floor-debate stage are often considerably different bills and resolutions than when first introduced. Most of the disparity between the number and content of bills introduced in Congress and bills which reach the floor for debate may be accounted for by the power of congressional committees and their ability to stop, impede, alter, modify, or report out unchanged legislation which is submitted to them. Hence, a study of congressional decision-making which concentrates on roll-call voting leaves out of consideration the important influences which congressional committees have on the kind of legislation which is likely to get through Congress.[3]

Recognizing this limitation, however, merely means that all influences on the legislative process are not being considered here. It does not mean that the conclusions reached in this study are therefore invalid. The bills which do reach the floor of Congress for debate and roll-call vote are often quite important pieces of legislation, and a majority vote, of course, is needed in each house for passage. Roll-call voting is an important stage in the legislative process, then, and interested citizens will be concerned with the outcome of the voting. How different congressmen representing different kinds of constituencies vote on these bills, therefore, ought to give us some clue as to the importance of constituency and other influences in the legislative process. These influences may be working in other important stages of legislative decision-making, but they will also be prominent at the voting stage.

Having said this, what is the relationship between roll-call votes of congressmen and their constituencies? Can certain patterns of voting be discerned which will aid us in the understanding of the representative process? What follows is an attempt to answer these questions.

[3] See, for example, Charles O. Jones, "The Role Of The Congressional Sub-Committee," *Midwest Journal of Political Science*, VI (November, 1962), 327–45; Richard Fenno, Jr., "The House Appropriations Committee as a Political System: The Problem of Integration," *American Political Science Review*, LVI (June, 1962), 310–24; Charles O. Jones, "Representation in Congress: The Case of the House Agriculture Committee," *American Political Science Review*, LV (June, 1961), 358–68; and Ralph K. Huitt, "The Congressional Committee: A Case Study," *American Political Science Review*, XLVIII (June, 1954), 340–65.

The Importance of Party

Studies of roll-call voting in Congress have tended to stress two factors: (1) the large amount of party cohesion in Congress on most issues, and (2) the importance of constituency factors in explaining deviations from party votes within parties.[4] These studies suggest that party is the single most important predictor of roll-call behavior, and that constituency factors explain most of the deviation from party votes.[5] For example, Turner suggests that:

> quantitative analysis of roll-call votes shows, contrary to majority opinion, that significant differences exist between our major parties. While it is true that American discipline falls short of that achieved in some European democracies, and is less effective than party discipline in the McKinley era in the United States, evidence of great party influence can still be found. Party pressure seems to be more effective than any other pressure on congressional voting. . . .[6]

The extent of party unity can be seen from an analysis of roll-call votes in various Congresses. In 1961, 58 per cent of the 320 roll calls in both the Senate and the House found a majority of Democrats opposing a majority of Republicans. In 1960, 1959, 1958, and 1957 the comparable percentages were 42, 50, 42, and 47, respectively.[7] Certainly, as Turner points out, this is less than might be found in European systems, but it does give some indication that political parties do provide a basis of cleavage in American politics.

However, taking 1961 as an example (in which 58 per cent of the roll-call votes were votes on which a majority of one party

[4] Julius Turner, *Party and Constituency: Pressures on Congress* ("The Johns Hopkins University Studies in Historical and Political Science," Series 69, No. 1 [Baltimore: The Johns Hopkins Press, 1951]); Duncan MacRae, Jr., *Dimensions of Congressional Voting,* "University of California Publications in Sociology and Social Institutions," Vol. I, No. 3 [Berkeley: University of California Press, 1958]), pp. 203–390; and David B. Truman, *The Congressional Party* (New York: Wiley, 1959). For an analysis of variability on issues, see MacRae, *op. cit.,* and Samuel C. Patterson, "Dimensions of Voting Behavior in a One-Party State Legislature," *Public Opinion Quarterly,* XXVI (Summer, 1962), 185–201.

[5] Other factors include leaders versus rank-and-file, and state delegations, see Truman, *op. cit.*

[6] Turner, *op. cit.,* p. 23.

[7] *Congressional Quarterly Weekly Report,* No. 49, 1961, p. 1929.

opposed a majority of the other party), this still leaves 42 per cent, 135 out of 320, of the roll-call votes without a majority of Democrats opposing a majority of Republicans. Also, the average Democratic and Republican representative in both the Senate and the House voted only about 70 per cent of the time in agreement with his party on the 185 roll-call votes in which a majority of one party opposed a majority of the other party.[8] This means that on 30 per cent of these votes, the average Democrat and Republican voted against the majority of his party.

How does one explain this degree of party unity within Congress? How does one account for the extent of party deviation among congressmen? This chapter will attempt to demonstrate a relationship between party membership of congressmen and constituency factors and to show how variation in such constituency factors influences congressional voting. It will attempt to demonstrate that differences between Democrats and Republicans are not merely a matter of party label or ideology (few really contend otherwise), but are rooted in basic differences in the kinds of constituencies from which Democrats and Republicans come. Many of these differences have already been examined in Chapter 2. The chapter will then go on to show that these constituency factors are also important in explaining intraparty differences in voting in Congress, but only by way of supporting the hypothesis that party voting patterns reflect constituency differences.

This analysis is rooted in the general theory described in Chapter 1. That is, people located in similar kinds of environments are likely to share similar attitudes, such as voting Democratic or Republican, and to differ in their attitudes from those who do not share similar environmental situations. Hence, we would expect Democratic and Republican congressmen to disagree on a number of important public policy questions, and that these party differences will be reflected in different environmental conditions between Democratic and Republican constituencies. That is, as we will attempt to demonstrate, differences in congressional voting between Democrats and Republicans also reflect differences in gross kinds of political pressures.

[8] *Ibid.*

Party and Constituency Differences on Public Policy

The first step in our analysis is to demonstrate voting differences between Democrats and Republicans on matters of public policy. We will concentrate, in most of what follows, on differences between Democrats and Republicans in the northern and border states, excluding the 101 southern Democrats and 5 southern Republicans of the Old Confederacy. It was found, on preliminary analysis of the data, that although southern congressmen did exhibit distinctly different voting patterns from northern congressmen (see Table 7.1), the gross constituency variables chosen for this analysis did not show a relationship with voting in Congress among the southern congressmen. Other variables than the ones chosen in this study will have to be employed to explain differences in southern congressional voting.

Our unit of analysis will be the House of Representatives, Eighty-seventh Congress, First Session. The findings in this chapter are, of course, limited by time (one Congress) and place (the House of Representatives). It is hoped that the findings and explanations reported here will stimulate further research on other legislative bodies.

The best single source describing differences between the voting records of Democrats and Republicans is the *Congressional Quarterly*. We will use three of its groupings of votes: the Kennedy Support Score on Domestic Policy (percentage support on fifty roll-call votes on matters of domestic policy which President Kennedy personally favored); the Kennedy Support Score on Foreign Policy (percentage support on fifteen roll-call votes on matters of foreign policy which President Kennedy personally favored); and the Larger Federal Role Support Score (percentage support on ten roll-call votes which would increase the federal government's role in various aspects of our economy and society, e.g., aid to education, housing, minimum wage).[9] Table 7.1 presents the voting of northern Democrats, southern Democrats, and northern Republicans on these three indices.

Table 7.1 shows striking differences in voting patterns between northern Democrats, southern Democrats, and northern

[9] *Congressional Quarterly Weekly Report*, Nos. 42, 45, 1961.

TABLE 7.1

Scores of Northern Democrats, Southern Democrats, and Northern Republicans on Three Series of Roll-Call Votes*

| Region and Party | Average Scores | | | Total |
	Kennedy Domestic Support %	Kennedy Foreign Support %	Larger Federal Role %	N
Northern Democrats	83.8	83.9	92.7	(163)
Southern Democrats	56.9	57.2	56.4	(101)
Northern Republicans	34.4	53.3	17.3	(168)

* Data compiled from the *Congressional Quarterly Weekly Report*, Nos. 42, 45, 1961.

Republicans. The average Kennedy Support Score on Domestic Policy for northern Democrats is 83.8 per cent, for southern Democrats, 56.9 per cent, and for northern Republicans, 34.4 per cent; on Foreign Policy, 83.9 per cent for northern Democrats, 57.2 per cent for southern Democrats, and 53.3 per cent for northern Republicans. Northern Democrats support a Larger Federal Role 92.7 per cent of the time, southern Democrats, 56.4 per cent, and northern Republicans, 17.3 per cent. In each case, the southern Democrats lie somewhere between the average scores of northern Democrats and Republicans.

The second step in our argument is to illustrate constituency differences between northern Democrats and northern Republicans. The variables we have chosen are socioeconomic status (percentage owner-occupied dwelling units), race (percentage non-white population), population density (average population per square mile), and place of residence (percentage urban).[10] We expect, and find, that northern Democrats tend to come from districts which have a smaller percentage owner-occupied dwelling units, a higher percentage non-white population, a higher average population per square mile, and a higher percentage

[10] Data from the *Congressional District Data Book, Districts of the 87th Congress* (U.S. Department of Commerce, Bureau of the Census [Washington, D.C.: Government Printing Office, 1961]) for the first three variables, and the *Congressional Quarterly Weekly Report*, No. 8, 1962, for percentage urban. The definition of "urban" is that used by the Bureau of the Census, 1960.

urban population than do northern Republicans. Table 7.2 presents these data.

TABLE 7.2

Comparison Between Northern Democrats and Northern Republicans on Four Constituency Variables*

| Region and Party | Mean Average of Constituency Variables | | | | |
	Owner-Occupied %	Non-White %	Pop./ Sq. Mile Av.	Urban %	Total N
Northern† Democrat	55.5	12.6	11,032	74.5	(163)
Northern Republican	67.1	3.8	1,667	65.1	(168)

*Data compiled from the *Congressional District Data Book, Districts of the 87th Congress* (U.S. Department of Commerce, Bureau of the Census [Washington, D.C.: Government Printing Office, 1962]), and the *Congressional Quarterly Weekly Report*, No. 8, 1962.
† Northern includes all but the eleven former Confederate states.

We now have grounds for saying that one of the reasons why northern Democrats vote differently from northern Republicans in the House of Representatives is that the congressmen from each party tend to represent different kinds of constituencies. Northern Democratic constituencies are more urban, more racially mixed, have a lower percentage of owner-occupied dwelling units, and have more people per square mile than northern Republican constituencies. In other words, factors which are usually associated with liberalism (urban, lower socio-economic status, non-white, and densely populated areas) are the factors which are, in fact, associated with the more liberal party. And, if we assume that Kennedy is a liberal and that his program submitted to Congress is a liberal program, Table 7.3 illustrates that each of these four characteristics is correlated with a more liberal voting record, even with party held constant.

Table 7.3 shows the following relationships for both northern Democrats and northern Republicans: The lower the percentage of owner-occupied dwelling units in the congressional districts, the higher the Kennedy Support Score on Domestic Policy; the higher the percentage non-white, population per square mile, and percentage urban, the higher the Kennedy Support Score on Domestic Policy. The correlations are smaller for Republicans than for Democrats, but all are in the predicted direction.

TABLE 7.3

Relationship Between Four Constituency Factors and Kennedy Support Score on Domestic Policy for Northern Democrats and Northern Republicans*

	Domestic Policy Score and Constituency Factors				
Region and Party	% Owner-Occupied ϕ†	% Non-White ϕ	Pop./ Sq. Mile ϕ	% Urban ϕ	Total N
Northern Democrats	—.13	.19	.23	.26	(163)
Northern Republicans	—.12	.08	.05	.20	(168)

* Data compiled from the *Congressional Quarterly Weekly Report*, No. 42, 1961, and No. 8, 1962, and the *Congressional District Data Book, Districts of the 87th Congress* (U.S. Department of Commerce, Bureau of the Census [Washington, D.C.: Government Printing Office, 1961]).
† The measure of association is the phi coefficient.

We can now sum up our argument to this point. First, northern Democrats have more liberal voting records than do Republicans. Second, Democrats tend to come from districts with larger proportions of characteristics which are generally associated with liberalism than do Republicans. Third, these constituency differences are associated with liberal voting records independent of political party. Hence, Democrats have more liberal voting records partially, at least, because they tend to come from more liberal constituencies.

Finally, our argument can be bolstered in the following way: We can combine the four constituency variables into a single index. This is done by splitting each constituency variable at the median and separating those constituencies that are above the median on none, one, two, three, and four of the variables (for percentage owner-occupied dwelling units, above the median means scoring low on this characteristic). This index is then related to the party affiliation of the incumbent representatives. We predicted that as the number of characteristics above the median increased, there would be a higher proportion of Democrats elected. Table 7.4 presents data testing this hypothesis.

The data in Table 7.4 illustrate the proposition that whether a Democratic or Republican congressman is elected from a constituency is in considerable measure related to the four gross constituency factors which we have been considering. With one

TABLE 7.4

**Northern Democrats and Republicans on Combined
Constituency Index***

Number of Characteristics above the Median	Party Democratic %	Republican %	Total N
0	38	62	(55)
1	43	57	(89)
2	37	63	(52)
3	53	47	(70)
4	74	26	(65)

*The point biserial correlation for these data is .23.

exception, as the number of characteristics above the median increases, the percentage of Democratic incumbents increases. At the extremes, of the fifty-five congressional districts which, relatively speaking, have the most conservative population characteristics, 62 per cent elected a Republican congressman in 1960. And, of the sixty-five congressional districts which, again relatively speaking, have the most liberal population characteristics, 74 per cent elected a Democratic congressman in 1960.

Not only do those districts we have defined as liberal tend to elect Democrats and those districts we have defined as conservative tend to elect Republicans, but these constituency differences have effects on the behavior of the particular Democrats and Republicans who are elected, as well. For example, combining, for purposes of this analysis, those constituencies whose scores were none, only one, or only two above the median as conservative constituencies, and those constituencies whose scores were three or all four above the median as liberal constituencies, among the Democrats who come from conservative districts, 25 per cent have a Kennedy Support Score on Domestic Policy of 90 per cent or better. Among the Democrats who come from liberal districts, 41 per cent have a Kennedy Support Score on Domestic Policy of 90 per cent or better. Similarly, among the Republicans who come from liberal districts, 72 per cent support Kennedy more than 30 per cent of the time; whereas among the Republicans who come from conservative districts, only 58 per cent score this high.

This contrast is made even stronger when we look at the differences in voting on a select group of issues on which a majority of Republicans sided with a majority of southern Democrats against a majority of northern Democrats. This is the so-called Conservative Coalition.[11] Among the Democrats who come from conservative districts, 81 per cent voted with the Conservative Coalition on at least one of these twenty-three issues. Among the Democrats who come from liberal districts, only 31 per cent ever voted with the coalition. Similarly, among the Republicans who come from liberal districts, 56 per cent voted with the Conservative Coalition at least 70 per cent of the time. Among the Republicans who come from conservative districts, 75 per cent voted with the coalition at least 70 per cent of the time.

We may conclude, then, that much of the difference in roll-call votes between northern Democrats and northern Republicans may be explained on the basis of relationships between certain constituency characteristics and tendencies to vote liberal or conservative (these relationships hold even with party held constant). The fact that liberal districts tend to produce Democrats and conservative districts, Republicans completes the argument.

Additional Speculation

We are also left with a speculative notion of this nature: It might be quite possible that the relationships between constituency factors, party affiliation of congressmen, and roll-call votes would be even higher than here indicated if we knew something of the congressman's perception of his district and what he considers to be his effective constituency.[12] Perhaps Democratic congressmen from the North tend to overrepresent the liberal elements within their constituencies because those are the ones which they perceive (and perhaps quite rightly) as being impor-

[11] *Congressional Quarterly Weekly Report*, No. 44, 1961.

[12] For a discussion of the importance of perception in the representative-constituency relationship, see Lewis A. Dexter, "The Representative and His District," *Human Organization*, XVI (Spring, 1957), 11–16. For initial data on the problem, see Warren E. Miller, "Policy Preferences of Congressional Candidates and Constituents," Paper delivered at the 196 Annual Meeting of the American Political Science Association, St. Louis, Missouri.

tant for their election and re-election. Similarly, it might be the case that Republican congressmen tend to overrepresent the conservative elements within their constituencies for the same reasons. This selective attention to groups within a constituency would help to explain why the correlation between gross constituency factors and party affiliation of the winning candidate is not stronger than here indicated. The fact that gross constituency variables explain as much as they do is noteworthy, but the addition of data about congressmen's perceptions of their constituencies and the probable differential attention to and access by some groups rather than others would help us to understand better the representative relationship between the congressman and his constituency.

A related point has to do with the "responsible parties" question. Turner has pointed out that because of the heterogeneous make-up of the parties, attempts to enforce a more rigid party line in Congress might have the effect of forcing many congressmen to take positions inconsistent with constituency influences. This, in Turner's view, would have the effect of reducing the strength of the party in those areas and increasing the number of one-party areas.[13] The data reported here are consistent with Turner's views. Democrats from conservative-type districts and Republicans from liberal-type districts do tend to vote more conservatively and liberally respectively than their party cohorts. Forcing a stricter party line on these congressmen might indeed affect their ability to please their own constituents, reduce their strength within their own constituencies, and increase the number of one-party districts.

One further note about the methodology used in this chapter: The measures and data employed are admittedly gross. This leaves a great deal of room for error. But, as far as possible, in choosing data and methods we have attempted to load the dice against the hypotheses rather than for them. For example, the states excluded from the analysis are the eleven former Confederate states only. Included in the definition of northern states are Kentucky, Oklahoma, and other border states. Similarly, we have used as our most important measure of voting differences

---

[13] Julius Turner, "Responsible Parties: A Dissent from the Floor," *American Political Science Review*, XLV (March, 1951), 143–52.

the Kennedy Support Score on Domestic Policy, an index which, if anything, would tend to maximize party differences over a wide range of issues because of the direct involvement in such issues by a Democratic President. And, third, the constituency variables included in this analysis are limited in number and, again, are of the grossest variety. Still, under all these limiting conditions, the major hypothesis of this chapter that voting differences between Democrats and Republicans reflect, at least in part, constituency differences between Democrats and Republicans is substantiated. Further, more specific, research into the relationship between constituency influence and congressional voting should help us to estimate more precisely how important such influence is in relation to other factors.

The Effect of the Particular
Incumbent on Congressional Voting*

Introduction

Chapter 7 was concerned with the relationships among party affiliations of congressmen, constituency differences between the parties, and the effects that such differences in constituencies have on congressmen's roll-call voting. We found that Democrats and Republicans do vote differently in Congress and that these party differences reflect underlying differences in the kinds of constituencies from which Democrats and Republicans come. We also found that all the members of the same party do not vote identically on matters of public policy, but that there is variation in voting within the parties as well as between them. These voting differences within parties, too, may be partially accounted for by the fact that liberal Democrats or Republicans tend to come from constituencies which are more liberal in their characteristics than do conservative Democrats or Republicans.

* This chapter is a revised version of an earlier paper, "The Importance of Individuality in Voting in Congress," *Journal of Politics*, II (May, 1963), 324–32. I would like to thank the editor of the *Journal of Politics* for permission to use much of the body of that paper.

Having shown that voting on matters of public policy in Congress may be explained on the basis of party and constituency differences, what role does this leave the particular man in office? That is, does it make a difference in congressional voting which particular Democrat and which particular Republican is representing a constituency? Can we discern individual differences in voting as well as party and constituency differences?

This chapter will be concerned with answering just such questions. However, before turning to this, let us put the questions in a proper context. We have already seen that many of the voting differences among congressmen may be explained on the basis of party and constituency differences. We should, therefore, not expect much individual difference in the voting performance of congressmen when party and constituency are held constant. In this regard, we agree with Turner's conclusion: "It appears, however, that these differences [in the voting behavior of congressmen after party affiliation has been held constant] are much more closely connected with differences in the constituencies than with differences in the personal characteristics of congressmen."[1]

Second, and this is merely an extension of the discussion at the beginning of Chapter 7, we will be concerned only with individual differences in congressional roll-call votes. The importance of particular representatives in other roles they play, such as in leadership positions, committee memberships, debates on the floor of the House, are not in question here. Whether, for example, any Speaker of the House could have won the fight to enlarge the Committee on Rules in 1961, or whether it was Speaker Rayburn's personal influence is an interesting question, but one which will not be answered here.[2] Whether any congressman could have defeated Representative Albert for the majority leadership of the Democratic party in 1962 as Congressman Bolling

---

[1] Julius Turner, *Party and Constituency: Pressures on Congress* ("The Johns Hopkins University Studies in Historical and Political Science," Series 69, No. 1 [Baltimore: The Johns Hopkins Press, 1951]), p. 172.

[2] See Hugh Douglas Price, "Race, Religion, and the Rules Committee: The Kennedy Aid-to-Education Bills," in Alan F. Westin, ed., *The Uses of Power: Seven Cases in American Politics* (New York: Harcourt, Brace, & World, 1962), pp. 13–20, for a discussion of the Rules Committee fight.

attempted to do is also an interesting question,[3] but we will be concerned with only one aspect of the congressman's behavior, his roll-call votes. This is an important part of his behavior, but it is only one part.

This chapter will attempt to show (1) that which particular Democrat or Republican holds office does affect congressional voting and (2) that these differences are independent of constituency differences. We shall examine the voting records of congressmen on the reciprocal trade issue from 1948 to 1958.[4] We shall select only the 306 congressional districts with one-party incumbency during this period (omitting those districts which had representatives from both parties) and divide these 306 districts into those with one and only one Republican representative during this period, those with more than one Republican representative (but only Republicans), those with one and only one Democratic representative, and those with more than one Democratic representative (but only Democrats). If, as predicted, it does make a difference which particular Democrat and which particular Republican is in office, then there should be a difference in the voting patterns on reciprocal trade legislation between those one-party districts with more than one incumbent during the period studied and those one-party districts with only a single incumbent. Differences in constituency factors which might be related to whether or not a constituency has elected more than one Democrat or Republican will be explored, and any that do show a relationship will be held constant.

[3] See Nelson W. Polsby, "Two Strategies of Influence: Choosing a Majority Leader, 1962," in Robert L. Peabody and Nelson W. Polsby, eds., *New Perspectives on the House of Representatives* (Chicago: Rand McNally, 1963), chap. ix.

[4] The *Congressional Quarterly Weekly Report*, No. 17, 1962, pp. 678–82. The *Congressional Quarterly* lists six roll-call votes on amendments to reciprocal trade legislation between 1948 and 1958 and shows how each congressional district voted on each amendment. The percentages in Table 8.1 are based on the number of districts which cast ballots in favor of more liberal reciprocal trade legislation all six times or against more liberal reciprocal trade legislation all six times, or had mixed votes (both for and against more liberal reciprocal trade legislation on at least one of the six roll calls). Tables 8.3 and 8.4 are based on percentage of districts with mixed votes only. The proportion of representatives who voted for more liberal reciprocal trade legislation on each of the roll calls studied was 44 per cent (1948), 61 per cent (1949), 43 per cent (1951), 46 per cent (1953), 51 per cent (1955), and 65 per cent (1958).

The Particular Incumbent Does Make a Difference

Table 8.1 presents findings which indicate that there is a difference in voting on reciprocal trade between constituencies with only one Republican versus those with more than one Republican, and those with only one Democrat versus those with more than one Democrat.

TABLE 8.1

Voting on Reciprocal Trade Between 1948 and 1958 among Constituencies with Only One Republican Vs. Those with More Than One Republican, and Those with Only One Democrat Vs. Those with More Than One Democrat*

Region, District Incumbent(s)	Vote on Reciprocal Trade			
	Consistently For %	*Consistently Against* %	*Mixed* %	*Total* N
North				
Same Republican	2	42	56	(43)
More Than One Republican	2	36	62	(88)
Same Democrat	74	3	23	(39)
More Than One Democrat	48	0	52	(40)
South†				
Same Democrat	58	2	40	(43)
More Than One Democrat	26	0	74	(53)

*Data compiled from the *Congressional Quarterly Weekly Report*, No. 17, 1962, pp. 678–82.
† The states defined as "South" are the eleven former Confederate states.

From Table 8.1 we can draw the following tentative conclusions:

1. Representatives from districts with only one Republican representative are more likely to have voting records consistently against liberal reciprocal trade amendments and are less likely to have mixed voting records (both for and against one or more of the six liberalizing amendments) than are those from districts having more than one Republican representative.

2. Representatives from districts with only one Democratic representative are more likely to have voting records consistently for liberal reciprocal trade amendments and are less likely to

have mixed voting records than are those from districts having more than one Democratic representative.

3. More generally, representatives from one-party districts which elected more than one representative during the period studied show a more variable voting pattern than those from one-party districts in which there was only one incumbent.

4. The largest variation in voting on reciprocal trade between one-party districts with only one incumbent and one-party districts with more than one incumbent is among southern Democrats (40 per cent of the southern Democratic districts with a single representative show a mixed voting pattern, whereas 74 per cent of the southern Democratic districts which elected more than one Democratic representative show a mixed voting record, a difference of 34 per cent).

5. The next largest variation is among the northern Democrats (23 per cent of the northern Democratic districts with a single representative show a mixed voting pattern as opposed to 52 per cent of the northern Democratic districts with more than one incumbent during this period, a difference of 29 per cent).

6. The smallest variation is among northern Republicans (56 per cent of the northern Republican districts with a single representative show a mixed voting record compared with 62 per cent of the northern Republican districts with more than one Republican incumbent, a difference of 6 per cent).

7. More generally (and more tentatively), the importance of the man himself on reciprocal trade roll-call votes in Congress during this period seems to vary both with party and with section of the country.

It is now important to investigate whether the variations in voting on reciprocal trade just shown between one-party districts with one incumbent and one-party districts with more than one incumbent during the period studied are due to differences in constituency factors which may distinguish between these two types of districts, or whether such voting variation may be attributed to the persons occupying the office. That is, before we can say that the voting variation just described is due to differences in the men holding office, we must first ascertain whether these differences might be a result of basic differences in constituency characteristics between one-party districts which elected a single incumbent during this period and one-party districts which elected more than one representative.

In order to provide a partial answer to this question, we examined differences in gross constituency factors among the three sets of districts (single- and multiple-incumbency districts among northern Republicans, northern Democrats, and southern Democrats). Four constituency variables were chosen: percentage non-white, competitiveness of district (number of elections [1952–1960] in which the percentage for the winning candidate was 60 or over), socioeconomic status (percentage owner-occupied dwelling units), and percentage urban.[5] Table 8.2 presents these data.

It can be seen from Table 8.2 that for Republicans, the gross constituency factors do not differentiate between one-party districts with only one Republican representative and one-party districts with more than one Republican representative. We may conclude, then, with regard to Republicans, that what differences there are in voting patterns on reciprocal trade between districts with one Republican incumbent and districts with more than one Republican are due, not to gross constituency factors, but to which Republican incumbent is holding office at the particular time. However, the voting variation which may be attributed to differences in incumbents is quite small (see Table 8.1 and proposition 6 which follows the table).

For northern Democrats, however, we do find gross constituency differences between one-party districts with one Democratic representative over the ten-year period studied and one-party districts with more than one Democratic incumbent. Do these differences in constituency factors help to explain the voting variation between single-incumbency districts and multi-incumbency districts among northern Democrats found in Table 8.1? Table 8.3 presents data bearing on this question.

Table 8.3 illustrates that even with the four constituency variables held constant (percentage non-white, competitiveness

[5] Data compiled from the *Congressional Quarterly Weekly Report*, No. 8, 1962, pp. 678–82, for per cent urban. The definition of urban is that of the Bureau of the Census, 1960. Data for the other three variables are compiled from the *Congressional District Data Book, Districts of the 87th Congress* (U.S. Department of Commerce, Bureau of the Census [Washington, D.C.: Government Printing Office, 1961]).

TABLE 8.2

Comparisons on Four Variables Between Constituencies with Only One Republican Vs. Those with More Than One Republican, and Those with Only One Democrat Vs. Those with More Than One Democrat*

Region, District, Incumbent(s)	10% or More Non-White %	Constituency Characteristics		50% or More Urban	
		Average No. of Elections over 60% Av.	50% or More Owner-Occupied Dwelling Units %	%	N
North					
Same Republican	5	2.41	93	70	(43)
More Than One Republican	6	2.46	93	71	(88)
Same Democrat	38	3.89	72	85	(39)
More Than One Democrat	50	3.60	60	80	(40)
South					
Same Democrat	86	4.83	93	44	(43)
More Than One Democrat	81	4.60	94	45	(53)

*Data compiled from the *Congressional Quarterly Weekly Report*, No. 17, 1962, pp. 678–82, and No. 8, 1962, pp. 285–86, and the *Congressional District Data Book, Districts of the 87th Congress* (U.S. Department of Commerce, Bureau of the Census [Washington, D.C.: Government Printing Office, 1962]).

TABLE 8.3

Northern Constituencies with Only One Democratic Representative and Those with More Than One Democratic Representative with Mixed Voting Records on Reciprocal Trade, with Four Variables Held Constant*

Constituency Characteristics	Northern Constituencies			
	Same Democrat		More Than One Democrat	
	%	N	%	N
Non-White				
Less Than 10%	33	(24)	70	(20)
10% or More	7	(15)	35	(20)
Competitiveness				
Less Than 5 Elections over 60%	41	(17)	71	(24)
All 5 Elections over 60%	10	(21)	25	(16)
Owner-Occupied				
Less Than 50%	18	(11)	25	(16)
50% or More	25	(28)	71	(24)
Urban				
Less Than 50%	33	(6)	75	(8)
50% or More	21	(33)	47	(32)

*Data compiled from the *Congressional Quarterly Weekly Report*, No. 17, 1962, pp. 678–82, and No. 8, 1962, pp. 285–86, and the *Congressional District Data Book, Districts of the 87th Congress* (U.S. Department of Commerce, Bureau of the Census [Washington, D.C.: Government Printing Office, 1961]).

of district, percentage owner-occupied dwelling units, and percentage urban), one-party northern Democratic districts with more than one incumbent show a more variable voting pattern on reciprocal trade than do one-party northern Democratic districts with only one incumbent during the period studied. In each case in Table 8.3, those districts with more than one incumbent had a higher percentage of mixed votes (both for and against one or more of the six amendments) than those districts with only one incumbent.

Table 8.3 also illustrates, however, that the amount of variation in voting patterns between single-incumbency and multiple-incumbency districts varies with several of the constituency factors. For example, among northern Democratic districts with less than 50 per cent owner-occupied dwelling units, the variation between single- and multiple-incumbency districts is 7 per cent, but among northern Democratic districts with more than 50 per cent owner-occupied dwelling units, the variation between the two types of districts is 46 per cent. Although one must be extremely cautious in interpreting these differences, the data suggest that the importance of the particular incumbent in office in determining the vote on reciprocal trade legislation varies not only with party and section of the country (as suggested in Table 8.1), but also, among northern Democrats, with competitiveness of the district and socioeconomic status of the community (the two most striking differences in Table 8.3).

However, we can conclude, with regard to northern Democrats, that even with certain constituency factors held constant, there is still considerable variability in voting on reciprocal trade legislation which may be attributed to the particular incumbent in office, although this variability in voting itself varies among different types of constituencies.

With regard to southern Democrats, we see from Table 8.2 that there are two constituency characteristics which might explain the variation in voting on reciprocal trade between single- and multiple-incumbency districts. As shown in Table 8.4, however, neither of these characteristics, when held constant, changes the basic finding of larger voting variation on reciprocal trade legislation among districts with more than one incumbent as opposed to districts with a single incumbent. In each case, those districts with more than one incumbent Democrat have a higher percentage of mixed votes than districts with a single incumbent.

We may conclude, then, with regard to southern Democrats, that there is considerable variation in voting on reciprocal trade which may be attributed to the particular incumbent in office, although again, as with northern Democrats, this variability itself varies with certain gross constituency factors.

Conclusions

We have attempted, in this chapter, to devise a way to separate party, constituency, and personal influences on congressional voting, and to ascertain the conditions under which the last is important in determining the position a district takes, through its congressman, on legislation. Roll-call votes on re-

TABLE 8.4

Southern Constituencies with Only One Democratic Representative and Those with More Than One Democratic Representative with Mixed Voting Records on Reciprocal Trade, with Two Variables Held Constant*

Constituency Characteristics	Southern Constituencies			
	Same Democrat		More Than One Democrat	
	%	N	%	N
Non-White				
Less Than 10%	17	(6)	90	(10)
10% or More	43	(37)	70	(43)
Competitiveness				
Less Than 5 Elections over 60%	50	(4)	73	(11)
All 5 Elections over 60%	38	(39)	74	(42)

*Data compiled from the *Congressional Quarterly Weekly Report*, No. 17, 1962, pp. 678–82, and the *Congressional District Data Book, Districts of the 87th Congress* (U.S. Department of Commerce, Bureau of the Census [Washington, D.C.: Government Printing Office, 1961]).

ciprocal trade amendments between 1948 and 1958 were chosen as the dependent variable. If the particular incumbent holding office does make a difference in how the constituency is recorded in roll-call votes, then there should be a difference in voting on reciprocal trade between those districts which had only one incumbent and those districts which elected more than one incumbent of the same party during this ten-year period. Constituency variables which were related to differences in single- versus multiple-incumbency districts were held constant.

The data presented in this paper lend support to the following conclusions:

A. Which particular incumbent is in office does make a difference in how a congressional district will be recorded on legislative roll-calls.

B. However, the amount of variation in legislative roll-call votes which may be attributed to the particular incumbent varies with several factors:

    1. The party: The importance of the particular incumbent on legislative roll-calls is greater for Democrats than for Republicans (Table 8.1).

2. The region: The importance of the particular incumbent on legislative roll-calls is greater for southern Democrats than for northern Democrats (Table 8.1).

    a. Competitiveness: Among northern Democrats, the importance of the particular incumbent is greater in districts which are more competitive than in districts which are less competitive (Table 8.3).

    b. Owner-occupied dwelling units: Among northern Democrats, the importance of the particular incumbent is greater in districts which are better-off economically than in districts which are less well-off economically (Table 8.3).

    c. Non-white population: Among southern Democrats, the importance of the particular incumbent is greater in districts which have a smaller percentage non-white population than in districts with a larger percentage non-white population (Table 8.4).

    d. Competitiveness: Among southern Democrats, the importance of the particular incumbent is greater in districts which are less competitive than in districts which are more competitive (Table 8.4).

One additional important difference is shown in the above conclusions. For northern Democrats, the importance of the particular incumbent is greater in districts which are more competitive than in districts which are less competitive (2 a.). For southern Democrats, just the reverse is true—the importance of the particular incumbent is greater in districts which are less competitive than in districts which are more competitive (2 d.). This difference may be explained in the following manner: For northern Democrats, competitiveness of district is related to heterogeneity of constituents within the district. That is, the more varied the population within the district, the more competitive the district is likely to be (see Chapter 9). In these northern, competitive, Democratic districts, different people running on the Democratic ticket may appeal to a number of different groups in fashioning their electoral coalition. That is, in these districts, there is a larger range of alternative coalitions than in less competitive districts. Hence, the particular winning coalition is likely to vary considerably from man to man.

In the southern Democratic districts, however, non-competitiveness in the general election is also likely to mean relatively strong competition for the nomination within the Democratic party at the primary election.[6] This high degree of competition within the party is likely to foster attempts by the candidates to distinguish themselves from each other on a personal basis. Hence, in the South, we would expect to find that those from less competitive districts would be more likely to vary on individual characteristics than those from competitive districts.

The data analyzed in this chapter, however, bear out the general hypothesis that which particular Democrat and which particular Republican is elected to office does have an impact on voting in Congress. And, perhaps more important, the personal influence of the incumbent varies by party, region of the country, and certain constituency factors within region of the country.

[6] See V. O. Key, Jr., *Southern Politics in State and Nation* (New York: Knopf, 1949).

9

Competitiveness, Constituency Factors, and Roll-Call Votes

Introduction

We have already seen, in Chapter 2, how competitiveness of congressional districts relates to voting by the general population. Generally, the more competitive the district, the higher the voting turnout. In this chapter we will explore the relationship between competition for office and voting by congressmen. The major question to be pursued is, do congressmen from competitive districts vote differently from congressmen from safe districts?

A number of studies of state legislatures have suggested a relationship between the degree of party competition within districts and roll-call voting. Patterson, in a study of the Wisconsin Assembly, found that "mavericks" (those who vote with their party least) tend to come from marginal (close, competitive) districts.[1] Dye, in a similar study of the Pennsylvania General Assembly, found the same relationship. The more competitive the district, the less the party voting.[2] MacRae, in an

[1] Samuel C. Patterson, "The Role of the Deviant in the State Legislative System: The Wisconsin Assembly," *Western Political Quarterly*, XIV (June, 1961), 460–73.

[2] Thomas R. Dye, "A Comparison of Constituency Influences in the Upper and Lower Chambers of a State Legislature," *Western Political Quarterly*, XIV (June, 1961), 473–81.

investigation of the Massachusetts House of Representatives, suggests two relationships: (1) legislators from less competitive districts are more likely to take extreme positions on issues than legislators from marginal districts; and (2) representatives whose previous election margins were close tend to reflect constituency characteristics in their votes more closely than do those with wider margins.[3] Patterson, in a study of the Oklahoma Assembly, found that competitiveness of the district was directly related to support for the governor's program (although not related to any other series of roll-call votes).[4]

The purpose of this analysis is to see whether these hypotheses about state assemblies are true at the national level and to add further information about the relationship between competitiveness of districts and roll-call voting in the United States House of Representatives. We will also be concerned with factors other than roll-call votes which may be related to competitiveness of districts, factors which help to explain why some districts are more competitive than others.

Relationship Between Competitiveness of Districts and Roll-Call Votes

Our first task is to show a relationship between competitiveness of districts and roll-call votes. Since political party affiliation has been shown to be such an important variable in explaining congressional behavior,[5] its effects will be held constant.

[3] Duncan MacRae, Jr., "The Relation Between Roll Call Votes and Constituencies in the Massachusetts House of Representatives," in Heinz Eulau, Samuel J. Eldersveld, and Morris Janowitz, eds., *Political Behavior* (Glencoe, Ill.: Free Press, 1956), pp. 317–24. See also, Duncan MacRae, Jr., *Dimensions of Congressional Voting* ("University of California Publications in Sociology and Social Institutions" [Berkeley: University of California Press, 1958]), I, 203–390.

[4] Samuel C. Patterson, "Dimensions of Voting Behavior in a One-Party State Legislature," *Public Opinion Quarterly*, XXVI (Summer, 1962), 185–201.

[5] See Chapter 7; Julius Turner, *Party and Constituency: Pressures on Congress* ("The Johns Hopkins University Studies in Historical and Political Science," Series 69, No. 1 [Baltimore: The Johns Hopkins Press, 1951]); and David B. Truman, *The Congressional Party* (New York: Wiley, 1959).

On the basis of five elections for the United States House of Representatives (1952 to 1960), northern congressional districts[6] were divided into the following categories:[7]

Republican

1. Districts in which the Republican party won all five elections by 60 per cent or more of the vote (N = 23)
2. Districts in which the Republican party won all five elections by at least 55 per cent of the vote, but less than 60 per cent (N = 40)
3. Districts in which the Republican party won all five elections, but at least one election was by under 55 per cent of the vote (N = 66)
4. Districts in which the present incumbent is a Republican (1960 election), but in which the Democratic party won at least once (N = 33)

Democratic

5. Districts in which the present incumbent is a Democrat (1960 election), but in which the Republican party won at least once (N = 49)
6. Districts in which the Democratic party won all five elections, but at least one election was by under 55 per cent of the vote (N = 29)
7. Districts in which the Democratic party won all five elections by at least 55 per cent of the vote, but less than 60 per cent (N = 14)
8. Districts in which the Democratic party won all five elections by 60 per cent or more of the vote (N = 36)

These eight classifications represent a continuum from safest Republican (1) to safest Democratic (8). One interesting side observation which can be drawn from this classification is that, even excluding southern and border states, only 28 per cent of

[6] Sixteen southern and border states are excluded. This is due not only to the lack of competitiveness of congressional districts in most of these states (only 11 of the 144 districts have been represented by both parties in the period from 1952 to 1962), but also to factors which make voting by Democrats in these states somewhat different from voting by northern Democrats. See Chapter 2.

[7] Data from the *Congressional Quarterly Almanac* (Washington, D.C.: Congressional Quarterly, Inc., 1961), Vol. XVII.

the districts have been represented by members of both parties in this ten-year period.[8]

To test the relationships between competitiveness of districts and congressional voting in the House of Representatives which were suggested in the Introduction, we have chosen five sets of roll-call votes as compiled by the *Congressional Quarterly* (Eighty-seventh Congress, First Session): Partisan Support (percentage support for one's party on forty roll-call votes on which a majority of northern Democrats and a majority of southern Democrats opposed a majority of Republicans); Party Unity (percentage support for one's party on fifty-eight roll-call votes on which a majority of Democrats opposed a majority of Republicans); the Kennedy Support Score on Domestic Policy (percentage support on fifty roll-call votes on matters of domestic policy which President Kennedy personally favored); the Larger Federal Role Support Score (percentage support on ten roll-call votes which would increase the federal government's role in various aspects of our economy and society, e.g., aid to education, housing, minimum wage); and the Conservative Coalition Support Score (percentage support on twenty-three roll-call votes on which a majority of Republicans sided with a majority of southern Democrats against a majority of northern Democrats).[9] Table 9.1 presents data relating degree of competitiveness of the parties with voting on these five indices.

With the data in Table 9.1 we can now compare the propositions relating competitiveness of districts to roll-call votes in state legislatures with similar propositions about the United States House of Representatives.

The first hypothesis we will discuss is that suggested by Patterson and Dye: The more competitive the district, the less likely the representative will vote with his party.[10] This proposition follows from the notion that representatives from competitive districts, because of the greater heterogeneity of their constituents, are more likely than representatives from safe districts to find the interests of some of their constituents in conflict with party pressures. Because their electoral margins are close, these

---

[8] See Chapter 5 for a further discussion.
[9] *Congressional Quarterly Weekly Report*, Nos. 42, 44, 45, 47, 49, 1961.
[10] Patterson, *op. cit.*, and Dye, *op. cit.*

TABLE 9.1

Support on Five Series of Roll-Call Votes and Degree of Party Competition*

| Degree of Party Competition | Partisan Support | | Party Unity | | Roll-Call Vote Series | | | | | |
| | | | | | Kennedy Domestic Support | | Larger Federal Role | | Conservative Coalition | |
	%	Rank	%	Rank	%	Rank	%	Rank	%	Rank
Republican										
1	77.6	1	78.0	1	29.8	1	10.6	1	79.3	1
2	74.5	3	73.2	3	34.0	2	16.5	2	74.0	3
3	66.8	4	70.7	4	35.8	4	20.6	4	71.1	4
4	77.1	2	76.2	2	34.1	3	17.4	3	78.3	2
Democratic										
5	86.6	5	85.0	5	86.2	8	93.4	5	14.4	5
6	82.6	8	80.9	8	81.8	5	93.6	6	12.2	6
7	85.7	6	84.3	6	84.3	6	94.3	7	8.6	8
8	83.3	7	83.3	7	85.0	7	95.0	8	9.7	7

*Data compiled from *Congressional Quarterly Weekly Report*, Nos. 42, 44, 45, 47, and 49, 1961.

representatives will feel the need to submit to these pressures and hence will be less likely to vote with their party.

Using the Partisan Support and Partisan Unity scores from Table 9.1 as measures of party voting, we find the proposition that representatives from competitive districts vote less often with their party than representatives from safe districts to be partially false for Republicans, and completely false for Democrats. For Republicans, both Partisan Support and Party Unity decrease as competitiveness of the districts increases, *with the exception of the most competitive districts*. The least competitive Republican districts (1) do have the highest amount of party voting (77.6 and 78.0 per cent), and this party voting decreases as competitiveness increases, but the most competitive districts (4) score almost as high on Partisan Support and Party Unity as do the least competitive districts (77.1 and 76.2 per cent). We will return to the explanation of this exception a little later in the chapter.

For the Democrats, we do not even find the least competitive districts (8) having the highest party voting. On both the Partisan Support and Party Unity scores, the highest party voting (86.6 and 85.0 per cent) is found in the most competitive districts (5). Further, the data indicate no consistent relationship between degree of party competition and amount of party voting for the Democrats.

The hypothesis, then, that competitive districts exhibit less party voting than less competitive districts appears to be true for the Republicans (with one exception to be explained), but not true for the Democrats. The findings for the Democrats need to be explained on the basis of a theory different from that explaining the findings for the Republicans (that those from competitive districts will be more likely to find constituency pressures incongruent with party pressures and, because of the closeness of the election, they will vote with the constituency pressures and against the party). For the Democrats, a theory consistent with the findings is that representatives who find themselves in a conflict of pressures from their constituents (and those from competitive districts are more likely to be in conflict than those from safe districts) will solve the conflict by voting with the party or by voting their own personal convictions. Data from the last chapter indicate that Democrats from competitive districts are more likely to vote their own convictions than Democrats from safe districts. This is one way of solving the problem of how to vote when put in cross-pressures. The other way is to vote for the party. Data from this chapter indicate that this is also a strategy pursued by Democrats from competitive districts.

The second hypothesis which will be tested using data on the national House of Representatives is suggested by MacRae: The more competitive the district, the less likely are representatives to take extreme stands on matters of public policy.[11] This proposition follows from the theory that those from competitive districts will be more likely to have interests in their constituencies pushing in contrary directions. These representatives are more likely to pursue a moderate, middle-of-the-road strategy in the hopes of pleasing as many of the interests as possible. Representatives from safe districts, however, are also likely to be from relatively more homogeneous districts in which the pressures will be more likely to lead in one direction. Hence, they will be more likely to take extreme stands on issues.

We will interpret MacRae's hypothesis to mean, at the national level, that Republicans from competitive districts should be less conservative than Republicans from safe districts, and that Democrats from competitive districts should be less liberal than Democrats from safe districts. Using the Kennedy Support, Larger Federal Role, and Conservative Coalition Support scores as measures of liberal-conservative stands on issues, we find that the proposition is true for both Republicans (with one exception on each of the voting indices) and Democrats. Those Republicans who are most conservative come from the least competitive districts. As competitiveness of districts increases, conservatism decreases. The exceptions will be discussed below.

For the Democrats we find, generally, that the more competitive the districts, the less liberal the voting record. The major exception is on the Kennedy Support Score. The most competitive districts show the most support for the President's program. This exception, however, may be explained on the basis of another of Patterson's findings mentioned above. Patterson found, in the Oklahoma Assembly, that competitive districts were more

[11] MacRae, "The Relations Between Roll Call Votes . . .," *op. cit.*

likely to support the governor's program.[12] This, according to our data, is true for the most competitive districts.

Generally, however, the proposition that representatives from competitive districts are less likely to take extreme stands on issues than representatives from safe districts is confirmed. For both Republicans and Democrats, the more competitive the districts, the less likely are straight conservative or liberal positions.

The third hypothesis to be discussed is also suggested by MacRae: The more competitive the district, the more likely constituency preferences will be reflected in legislative roll-call votes.[13] Although the data in Table 9.1 cannot be used to test this hypothesis at the national level, we would expect, on the basis of the previous discussion, that this hypothesis would be false. Rather, we would expect congressmen from relatively more homogeneous, safe districts to reflect constituency opinion more than those from relatively heterogeneous, competitive districts. Data from the Survey Research Center's study of the House of Representatives support this theory. Miller reports that congressmen from safe districts are more likely to represent district opinion than congressmen from competitive districts, in direct contradiction to MacRae's hypothesis.[14] It is difficult, however, to tell whether these differences reflect differences in the methodologies in investigating these relationships or actual differences between the Massachusetts Assembly and the national House of Representatives.

Relationship Between Constituency Factors and Competitiveness of Districts

It is clear from our discussion to this point that degree of competitiveness of legislative districts does make some difference in the way congressmen vote. Although little relationship was found between competitiveness and party voting, representatives from more competitive districts (for both Democrats and

---

[12] Patterson, *op. cit.*

[13] MacRae, "The Relation Between Roll Call Votes . . .," *op. cit.*

[14] Warren E. Miller, "Majority Rule and the Representative System," Paper delivered at the 1962 Annual Meeting of the American Political Science Association, Washington, D.C., September 5–8, 1962.

Republicans) were shown to be less extreme in their voting than representatives from safe districts.

Having shown that competitiveness of districts does make some difference in legislative voting, we can now ask a second question, one which has not, as yet, been answered by others: Are there any factors, such as constituency characteristics, which will help to explain the relationship already established between competitiveness of congressional districts and roll-call votes? That is, how do we explain the fact that some congressional districts are more competitive than others, and how would such an explanation affect the relationship between competitiveness and roll-call votes?

To answer these questions, four constituency factors were chosen: race (percentage non-white), socio-economic status (percentage owner-occupied dwelling units), residence (percentage urban), and population density (average population per square mile).[15]

Table 9.2 presents data testing the hypothesis that as population characteristics of congressional districts vary, so too does competitiveness of the districts.

Table 9.2 provides some interesting and important information. Generally speaking, as congressional districts increase in percentage non-white (one exception), percentage urban (one exception), and population per square mile (two exceptions), and decrease in percentage owner-occupied dwelling units (one exception), they become less Republican and more Democratic. The Spearman Rank Order Correlation Coefficient for each of the above generalizations are, respectively, .86, .86, .83, and .93. For the Democrats, the relationship between constituency factors and competitiveness of the districts is nearly perfect. That is, as those districts with Democratic incumbents increase in percentage non-white, percentage urban, and average population per square mile, and decrease in percentage owner-occupied dwelling units, they also become less competitive.

For Republicans, however, the most competitive districts prove to be exceptions to the generalizations established above between

---

[15] *Congressional District Data Book, Districts of the 87th Congress* (U.S. Department of Commerce, Bureau of the Census [Washington, D.C.: Government Printing Office, 1961]); and the *Congressional Quarterly Weekly Report*, No. 8, 1962.

TABLE 9.2

**Competitiveness of Congressional Districts and Four
Constituency Characteristics***

| Degree of Party Competition | Constituency Characteristics | | | | | | | |
| | Average Non-White | | Average Owner-Occupied | | Average Urban | | Average Population Per Square Mile | |
	%	Rank	%	Rank	%	Rank	Av.	Rank
Republican								
1	3.26	2	71.1	1	63.7	2	834	2
2	4.02	3	65.7	3	67.0	3	2107	3
3	4.46	4	65.4	4	69.7	4	2787	4
4	3.11	1	68.9	2	56.5	1	471	1
Democratic								
5	5.84	5	63.3	5	72.3	5	7295	5
6	8.45	6	56.0	6	78.1	6	9107	6
7	10.28	7	46.4	7	83.5	7	30475	8
8	23.67	8	41.7	8	90.8	8	25809	7

*Data compiled from the *Congressional District Data Book, Districts of
the 87th Congress* (U.S. Department of Commerce, Bureau of the Census
[Washington, D.C.: Government Printing Office, 1961] and the *Congressional Quarterly Weekly Report*, No. 8, 1962.

constituency factors and competitiveness of districts. For Republicans, the most competitive districts rank lowest in percentage non-white, lowest in percentage urban, lowest in average population per square mile, and second highest in percentage owner-occupied dwelling units. In other words, the most competitive Republican districts are rural, white, low density, high home ownership districts—in short, farm districts. V. O. Key, Jr., and Angus Campbell *et al.* provide an explanation for this deviation from otherwise almost perfect rank order correlations. Key suggests that it is the middle-range towns and cities (10,000 to 50,000) which are the most conservative on matters of public policy, not the small towns and rural areas.[16] Hence, as Table 9.2 indicates, it is the districts with "middle-range" urban characteristics which are safest for the Republicans. Campbell *et al.* suggest that farmers have a higher variation in direction of vote (that is, switching back and forth between Democrats and Republicans) than any other occupational group.[17] This conclusion

[16] V. O. Key, Jr., *Public Opinion and American Democracy* (New York: Knopf, 1961), chap. v.
[17] Angus Campbell, Philip E. Converse, Warren E. Miller, and Donald E. Stokes, *The American Voter* (New York: Wiley, 1960), chap. xv.

is also supported in Table 9.2. It is the rural areas that are the most competitive Republican districts.

These findings also help us to explain the Republican exceptions which were noted in Table 9.1. In each case in Table 9.1, the Republican group which deviated from the rankings was number four, the most competitive group of districts. This is exactly the same group which is also deviating in Table 9.2. Hence, generalizing from Tables 9.1 and 9.2, the representatives from the most competitive Republican districts tend to have high Partisan Support and Party Unity scores, and tend to be more conservative in their legislative voting (exceptions from the general rule) because they represent constituencies whose characteristics support the deviation from the urban pattern.

We can now summarize the argument to this point. For both Democrats and Republicans, there is a close association between competitiveness of the districts and extreme stands taken on issues. For Democrats, the less competitive the districts, the more liberal their voting records. The major exception is that Democrats from the most highly competitive districts are the most likely to support the President's program. For the Republicans, the less competitive the districts, the more conservative their voting records. However, for the Republicans, the most competitive districts are exceptions to this rule.

There is also a close association between certain constituency factors and competitiveness of the districts. For Democrats, as constituencies increase in percentage non-white, percentage urban, and population per square mile, and decrease in percentage owner-occupied dwelling units, there is a decrease in competitiveness of the districts. There are no major exceptions to this generalization. For the Republicans, as constituencies decrease in percentage non-white, percentage urban, and population per square mile, and increase in percentage owner-occupied dwelling units, there is a decrease in competitiveness of the districts. The major exception to this generalization is that the most competitive Republican districts are the farm areas.

We can, on the basis of the above findings, come to certain general conclusions about the relationships between constituency factors, competitiveness of districts, and roll-call votes. First, there is a relationship between competitiveness of districts and roll-call votes. However, much of this relationship may be due to the fact that there is also a relationship between certain constituency factors and competitiveness of the districts. Generally (the exceptions have already been noted), as Republican districts decrease in competitiveness, they increase in conservative voting, and as Democratic districts decrease in competitiveness, they increase in liberal voting. However, it is also true that as Republican districts become less "urban" (using this word to include all four constituency characteristics), they become less competitive (excluding farm areas), and as Democratic districts become more "urban," they become less competitive.

We would then expect, on the basis of these two sets of relationships, that there would also be a close association between constituency factors and roll-call votes. This we have already shown to be the case in Chapter 7.[18] The more "urban" the district (again using this word to include all four constituency characteristics), the more liberal the voting record of the representative. Conversely, the less urban the district, the more conservative the voting record of the representative. The most important independent effects of competitiveness seem to be illustrated in the exceptions to these generalizations. For example, although Republican competitive districts are the least urban on constituency variables, they are not the most conservative on roll-call votes, indicating either an independent effect of competitiveness, less conservative views among farmers, or both. For the Democrats, the most competitive districts are most likely to support the President's program, again an exception to the general rule and illustrating the possible independent effect of competitiveness.

In general, however, the effect of competitiveness of districts, independent from constituency factors, appears to be quite limited. Rather, lack of competitiveness is a sign of greater homogeneity of constituency factors within the district which in turn is reflected in more liberal or conservative positions taken on issues (depending upon the direction of homogeneity) by representatives through their roll-call voting.

[18] See also, Turner, *op. cit.*; MacRae, "The Relation Between Roll Call Votes . . .," *op. cit.*; and MacRae, *Dimensions of Congressional Voting, op. cit.*

10

Summary and Conclusions

Democracies may be distinguished from dictatorships on the basis of the number of people who are allowed to participate in the decision-making process, the range of issues on which they may voice their opinions, and the impact that their participation may have on the making of public policy. This book has attempted to investigate various important relationships between participation in the political process, representative government, and the outcomes of public policy.

In Part I we examined the election process and attempted to answer a number of questions centering on the problem of who participates in the political process and the impact that such participation has for other parts of the political system. We found in Chapter 2, for example, that participation in elections varies with the kinds of people who are located within congressional constituencies, and that such variation also helps to explain why Democrats vote less than do Republicans, and why southerners vote less than northerners. In Chapter 3, we examined whether low participation in the political system is likely to result in instability of government, and tentatively concluded that because low participators are also likely to be less democratically oriented in their values than high participators, and because low participators are relatively stable in their low rates of voting, such apathy as exists is healthy for the political system.

In Chapters 4 and 5, we examined strategies and tactics in election campaigns to ascertain why Democrats are likely to win in some constituencies and Republicans in others, and how which party wins is influenced by factors of party identification, issues, candidate appeal, and whether the election takes place in a presidential or non-presidential year.

In Part II of this book, we turned to another aspect of the representative system, the relationship between a representative and his constituency. We found in Chapter 6, for example, that both institutional arrangements and election rules help to determine the general liberalism-conservatism of a representative institution. We found that the Senate is a more liberal institution than the House of Representatives on many (though not all) public policy issues. This greater liberalism in the Senate was explained on the bases that leaders are more conservative than non-leaders and that the House is more hierarchically organized than the Senate, as well as that House constituencies tend to overrepresent conservative interests.

In Chapter 7, we saw why Democrats tend to vote differently on questions of public policy than do Republicans. The explanation lies in the different kinds of people which Democrats represent as opposed to Republicans.

Chapter 8 was concerned with the question of the individual congressman himself and the impact that he has on public policy outcomes. Generally speaking, whether an incumbent votes his own convictions or not varies with the kind of constituency from which he comes, his party affiliation, and section of the country.

In Chapter 9, we explored the relationship between competitiveness of districts and congressional voting, and found that how competitive a district is does have some impact on how a congressman votes. Because competitive districts tend to be more heterogeneous than safe districts in the kinds of people who are represented, congressmen from competitive districts are less likely to take extreme positions on issues. We also found that safe districts tend to be more homogeneous in population characteristics than competitive districts, and that this higher degree of homogeneity is likely to result in a closer relationship between the preferences of the constituents and voting by the congressman. Especially among Democrats, those from competitive districts are placed in conflict situations and are more likely to solve these conflicts by voting with the party or voting their own personal convictions.

The theory underlying all of these chapters is that, in democratic systems, there will be a number of pressures on representatives to conform to the opinions and preferences of those who elected them. Not only will these pressures be overtly expressed in elections and through pressure group activity, but they will also be anticipated by the congressman in his actions to avoid their overt expression. We have attempted to ascertain under what conditions and to what extent these pressures are operating in a democratic system. Gross sociological, economic, and political factors were used as shorthand ways of getting at these pressures and anticipation of pressures.

Further, more specific research should help us to understand more precisely some of the questions raised in this book. However, it is hoped that what has been explored here will contribute to the better understanding of representative government.

Index

125